Palgrave Macmillan Memory Studies

Series Editors
Andrew Hoskins, University of Glasgow, Glasgow, UK
John Sutton, Department of Cognitive Science, Macquarie University,
Macquarie, Australia

The nascent field of Memory Studies emerges from contemporary trends that include a shift from concern with historical knowledge of events to that of memory, from 'what we know' to 'how we remember it'; changes in generational memory; the rapid advance of technologies of memory; panics over declining powers of memory, which mirror our fascination with the possibilities of memory enhancement; and the development of trauma narratives in reshaping the past. These factors have contributed to an intensification of public discourses on our past over the last thirty years. Technological, political, interpersonal, social and cultural shifts affect what, how and why people and societies remember and forget. This groundbreaking series tackles questions such as: What is 'memory' under these conditions? What are its prospects, and also the prospects for its interdisciplinary and systematic study? What are the conceptual, theoretical and methodological tools for its investigation and illumination?

Red Chidgey · Joanne Garde-Hansen

Museums, Archives and Protest Memory

palgrave
macmillan

Red Chidgey
Department of Culture, Media &
Creative Industries
King's College London
London, UK

Joanne Garde-Hansen
School of Media and Communication
University of Leeds
Leeds, UK

ISSN 2634-6257   ISSN 2634-6265   (electronic)
Palgrave Macmillan Memory Studies
ISBN 978-3-031-44477-7   ISBN 978-3-031-44478-4   (eBook)
https://doi.org/10.1007/978-3-031-44478-4

This Palgrave Macmillan imprint is published by the registered company Springer Nature Switzerland AG
The registered company address is: Gewerbestrasse 11, 6330 Cham, Switzerland

Paper in this product is recyclable.

Acknowledgements

This book is based on findings from the *Afterlives of Protest: The Protest Memory Research Network* (2018–2019), funded by the Arts and Humanities Research Council. This project was led by the University of Warwick (Grant Reference AH/R004889/1) in collaboration with King's College London, the University of Sussex, Loughborough University, the People's History Museum and Bishopsgate Institute. We would like to thank the partners, advisory committee and participants of the network, especially the members of the core organising team, Emily Keightley, Pollyanna Ruiz and Dion Georgiou. We express our gratitude to our advocates and collaborators: Janneke Geene, Michael Powell and Jenny Mabbott from the People's History Museum, Stefan Dickers from Bishopsgate Institute, Helen Ford from the Modern Records Centre at Warwick, Clare Watson at the Media Archive for Central England, Alan Rivett from Warwick Arts Centre, Jane Trowell from Platform, the Mass Observation Archive and Sparrows Nest. We thank colleagues who gave their precious time to discuss this topic with us in research interviews, in expert workshops and in symposia: Adam Jaffer, Alessandra Ferrini, Alex Buttersworth, Alison Atkinson-Phillips, Alison Ribeiro de Menezes, Amza Reading, Anastasia Kavada, Anna Feigenbaum, Anne Kaun, Ann Rigney, Cara Courage, Carmen Wong, Christina Flesher Fominaya, Christopher T. Boyko, Clara Vlessing, Corinna Gardner, D-M Withers, Damien Arness-Dalton, Elspeth (Billie) Penfold, Foteini Avaran, Gillian Whiteley, Gilson Schwartz, Hannah Awcock, Hazel Perry, Helen Antrobus, Jen Birks,

Jenny Wüstenberg, Joan Rutherford, Julia Downes, Karen Worcman, Karolina Szpyrko, Kate Antosik-Parsons, Kate Flannery, Kevin Ryan, Kirsty Patrick, Lizzie Thynne, Ludovica Roger, Marc Hudson, Margaretta Jolly, Mark Wilson, Matthew Allen, Matthew Lee, Mohamed El-Shewy, Morag Rose, Nicola Gauld, Nicky Hilton, Noam Tirosh, Nuria Querol, Orli Fridman, Paula Serafini, Pawas Bisht, Philipp Koellen, Polly Russell, Rachel Tavernor, Richard Martin, Rick Crownshaw, Rosanna Kennedy, Ruramisai Charumbira, Ruth Kinna, Sam Merrill, Sarah Briggs, Sarah Gensberger, Sarah Marsden, Sheetal Sharma, Shezara Francis, Sian Rees, Sophie Hyde, Stella Toonen, Winstan Whitter, Yifat Gutman, Zoe Strimpel. We thank Sheik Muhammad Nazeer Hussain Jaunoo for the design of our Protest Memory Network logo. Finally, a big thank you to the Cultural Memory class of King's College London who provided valuable feedback on a draft of Chapter Three, with special mention to the insights of Daniela Chaneva, Saiba Anand and Suyeon Lee, and to Jon Coburn for his insightful manuscript review. Above all, we thank the activists, cultural workers and heritage practitioners whose deep desire to document and amplify social justice work forms the basis of this book.

PRAISE FOR *MUSEUMS, ARCHIVES AND PROTEST MEMORY*

"This is a fascinating study of the challenges faced by cultural institutions in collecting and curating the memory of protest. Written in a clear and accessible manner which will appeal to a wide readership, it offers a compelling argument about the civic value of giving protest an afterlife. Highly recommended."

—Ann Rigney, *Utrecht University, The Netherlands*

"This short book enlivens memory as something that can spark protest and propel the commemoration, re-use and attempted management of its 'afterlives' by various players. Case studies of the Women's March and London's environmental river activisms offer rich models for readers seeking to understand the prefigurative political possibilities of activist collaborations with cultural institutions and for cultural workers alike. A terrific read."

—Kylie Message, *Australian National University, Australia*

CONTENTS

Abbreviations

AHD	Authorised Heritage Discourse
AI	Artificial Intelligence
AoP	Afterlives of Protest Research Network
AR	Augmented Reality
BI	Bishopsgate Institute
BLM	Black Lives Matter
CEO	Chief Executive Officer
Defra	Department of Environment, Food and Rural Affairs
DIY	Do It Yourself
DTP	Decolonize This Place
ERA	'Effra Redevelopment Agency'
EU	European Union
GLAM	Galleries, Libraries, Archives, Museums
IAWM	Internet Archive Wayback Machine
ICOM	International Council of Museums
IWD	International Women's Day
LGBTIQ+	Lesbian, Gay, Bisexual, Trans, Intersex, Queer, Questioning
LMA	London Metropolitan Archives
MoL	Museum of London
MoLD	Museum of London Docklands
OWS	Occupy Wall Street
PHM	People's History Museum
QR	Quick Response Codes
TERF	Trans-exclusionary Radical Feminist
UMVA	Umbrella Movement Visual Archive
V&A	Victoria and Albert Museum
VR	Virtual Reality

LIST OF FIGURES

LIST OF TABLES

CHAPTER 1

The Afterlives of Protest

Abstract We are currently witnessing an activist turn in civil society and its key institutions. This 'activist turn' speaks to renewed protest in the public sphere and growing expectations that cultural institutions should engage with activist demands and critiques. This includes the collection, curation and interpretation of protest heritage and a public declaration that cultural institutions are themselves advocates and activists on social issues. How do cultural institutions remember protest and connect protest legacies to historic and contemporary campaigns? This book demonstrates how protest memory, which we define as a form of civic knowledge, a set of cultural assets and an ethical domain in which cultural institutions are implicated, becomes a site of contestation for museums and archives to navigate reflexively, and for audiences to engage with critically. This chapter introduces the debates and methodologies of the *Afterlives of Protest Research Network* (2018–2019) which underpins our protest memory concept, framework and case studies. It further introduces the scope and structure of the book and provides a rationale for the value of approaching cultural institutions as important agents within the production and re-activation of protest sensibilities.

Keywords Social movements · Museums · Archives · Creative citizenship · Protest memory boom

© The Author(s), under exclusive license to Springer Nature
Switzerland AG 2024
R. Chidgey and J. Garde-Hansen, *Museums, Archives and Protest Memory*, Palgrave Macmillan Memory Studies,
https://doi.org/10.1007/978-3-031-44478-4_1

INTRODUCTION: THE PROTEST (MEMORY) BOOM

This book is located within a heightened moment of collecting, exhibiting and safeguarding activist voices and protest material culture in mainstream archives and museums. It does so through a particular lens: that of memory. We mobilise the concept of cultural memory to refer to the cultural presence of the past in the present. This provides an analytical frame for thinking carefully about multidirectional connections between the past, present and future, especially when composed through a commitment to social justice change.[1] Adopting a cultural memory lens, we contend, opens up significant new ways of investigating how contemporary and historic protest cultures are captured, memorialised and re-activated within settings of official memory construction, and the changes that happen as a result. To achieve these aims, we draw from the burgeoning field of activist memory studies as a new research trajectory that centres questions of resistance, activism and agency over a foundational concern with violence or trauma. We position these insights alongside critical museum, curatorial and archive studies, and in dialogue with concepts drawn from social movement, cultural and media studies.

This interdisciplinary and interprofessional project, which emerges as one of the first of its kind, speaks to the need to think both critically and pragmatically about how museums and archives can operate as "disobedient" institutions (Message 2018). It is our aim to provide a fresh take on the cultural value of remembering protest publicly and proactively, and to understand the management of protest memories and materials within mainstream arts and heritage settings. In doing so, we provide a close examination of how cultural institutions play a vital role in safeguarding and promoting civic protest memories as knowledge resources, albeit with a recognition of the myriad challenges and constraints in doing so.

There has been a veritable memory boom in archives and museums seeking to collect contemporary protest. Since 2011, archives have emerged in response to the Arab Spring pro-democracy movements (Della Ratta et al. 2020); the Occupy anti-capitalist movement (Gledhill 2012; Ross 2013; Erde 2014; Message 2020); and the Black Lives Matter racial justice movement (Rollason-Cass and Reed 2015; Salahu-Din 2019).[2] This is to cite only a handful of high-profile transnational protest movements that have attracted global media coverage and which have been documented via activist records, banners, photographs, videos, objects, wider material culture and born-digital and digitised records.

Museums, too, have centred historic and contemporary protest in their exhibitions, learning activities and public programmes, bringing these important materials to new audiences in a thematic interest with protest that shows no signs of slowing down.

Arguably such cultural institutions seek to demonstrate their relevance in the twenty-first century. Navigating new protest cultures can provide a means to respond to the needs, interests and demands of broader, especially marginalised and minoritised publics. The 'activist turn' in civil society and its key institutions speaks to the increasingly urgent call within the GLAM (Galleries, Libraries, Archives and Museums) sector for cultural institutions to lend their authority to the urgencies of planetary well-being and inequity redress (Caswell 2021; Chynoweth et al. 2020; Janes and Sandell 2019; Message 2014; Murawski 2021; Raicovich 2021).[3] To this we add that protest cultures enact a valuable form of creative citizenship; or what Ian Hargreaves calls "the application of creativity to civic purpose" (2016, p. 6). Protest cultures incubate new and diverse forms of creative collaboration, innovation and civic expression. With a particular focus on progressive and social justice-based protest cultures, we argue that these networks enact sites of 'hopeful creativity' for everyday citizens—whether such civic actors are legally recognised or not within the framework of the nation-state. To regard protest cultures as generating civic resources is to call into question the role that museums and archives can play in collecting and safeguarding such contentious heritage and valuable cultural assets.

When we invoke 'protest memory' in this book, we do so in a way that moves beyond a simple representational claim. To remember protest is not just to showcase the artefacts of protest movements in institutional memory settings. It is not solely to capture the ways in which social justice activism is publicly commemorated, silenced or forgotten. We invoke protest memory in a more intimate, implicated way. What does protest memory ask us to do, how does it move us? What kinds of ethical commitments does remembering protest necessitate? How does remembering protest call into account public cultural institutions? What forms of remembering can reinvigorate social justice claims, and what forms of remembering dull or mute protest sensibilities in the public sphere? How can we remember protest cultures well, with nuance, and care-fully?

The Afterlives of Protest Research Network

Underpinning this study is the *Afterlives of Protest Research Network* (Fig. 1.1) created by the authors in a collaboration between the University of Warwick, King's College London, the University of Sussex, Loughborough University, the People's History Museum and Bishopsgate Institute, and funded by the Arts and Humanities Research Council.[4] This research network sought to identify the ways in which protest memories move (spatially, temporally, medially and their velocity), how protest memories are engaged within cultural and heritage industries and sectors, and what practices organisational actors undertook as the custodians, curators and circulators of protest memory. Finally, exploring protest memory and its transmission as a form of social learning about past practices of resistance helped us to better understand how informal and formal protest knowledge is built and sustained.

To discuss this agenda, we held a series of workshops with museum professionals, archivists, artists, activists and academics between 2018 and 2019 on the themes of researching protest memory, mediating protest memory and curating protest memory. We completed the research network with a capstone conference held at the People's History Museum, Manchester during the exhibition *Disrupt? Peterloo and Protest,*

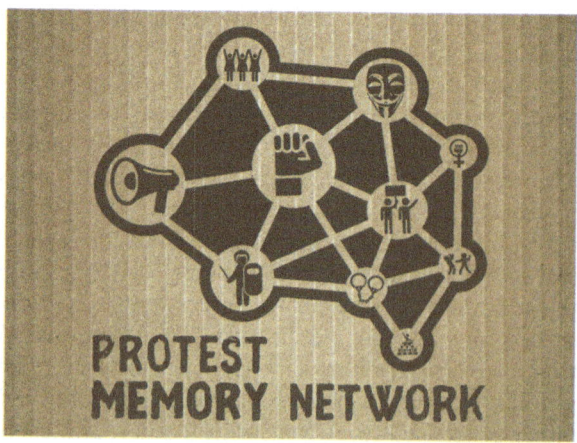

Fig. 1.1   The Afterlives of Protest Research Network Logo. Courtesy of Nazeer Hussain Jaunoo[5]

marking 200 years since the Peterloo Massacre in Manchester in 1819.[6] A concept of 'protest afterlives' underpinned our project from the outset. Protest afterlives refer to the remediation of previous protest acts, strategies, icons, images, activist processes and social movement knowledge through embodied, creative, informational and publicly shared means, sites and activities. As we have noted elsewhere, social movement memories and their cultural and social afterlives (online and offline) refer to "how the images, ideas and feelings of past liberation struggles become freshly available and transmissible in times not of their making" (Chidgey 2018, p. 1).

What was newly articulated through our research network, however, was that the very temporalities of this important memory work were being sped-up through the labour of museums and archive professionals and the present digital mediascape. There was no longer a delay of decades, or even centuries, between social movements being represented and remembered in archival and museum spaces. There was no waiting for bronze sculptors, plaque engravers or even high production value documentary filmmakers for protest memories to circulate in the public sphere. Contemporary social movement artefacts, oral histories and protest acts are now collected in *real time* through rapid response methodologies, as protest and public assemblies are themselves unfolding. This contemporaneity provides the focus of our book. As we suggest, museums and archives are uniquely positioned to create encounters between social movements and acts of protest, both historic and contemporary, and to enact deeper memory work surrounding the role, context and impact of activism and social change initiatives. Yet, none of this potential memory work is inevitable; as an emerging practice, it requires further academic and professional discussion.

To explore these issues, we utilised a range of social and arts-based methods to explore the topic of protest memory through a thoroughly arts and humanities-based perspective: starting from the recognition that protest itself is composed through embodied, affective encounters (Jasper 2018), and that cultural memory practices are creative and sensory (Seremetakis 1994). Our methods embraced memory walks through urban sites of historic protest; exploring the role of visual imagery in protest photos through quizzes; making protest badges with badge-making equipment used by local social movements; re-creating past protest news; and eating freshly baked empanadas with hand-stitched protest slogans on handkerchiefs to examine the role of food in the memories of Chilean women exiles in the UK (Ribeiro de Menezes and Wong 2018).

We listened to keynotes on issues of memory activism in Israel, Palestine and Brazil, where grassroots activists use memory and commemoration as key methods to enact social change (Gutman 2019; Schwartz 2019). We were critically introduced to community co-creation practices by museum scholars (Toonen 2019). Workshop participants then enacted the methodology of 'curatorial dreaming' (Butler and Lehrer 2016) to generate ideas of co-curated protest memory exhibitions, using toy museum kits and figures to discuss their project proposals (Fig. 1.2). From Damien Arness-Dalton (2019), a queer activist and Education and Engagement Officer at the Houses of Parliament, we learnt about Queerseum, a collective of activists, artists and queer educators who agitated for London to have its first permanent LGBTIQ+ museum to celebrate and share queer histories. This collective grabbed media headlines with their grassroots actions of placing pink filing cabinets spraypainted with the slogans 'Queer Museum. We Demand a Home' at the capital's queer landmarks. This action was to draw attention to "the millions of stories involving LGBT Londoners that sit hidden in museum archives" (Mills 2016).[7]

Speaking to issues of archival accessibility, activist and researcher Shezara Francis (2019), from Voices that Shake, discussed how institutional archives can act as sites of racial profiling and discomfort for people of colour (see Chilcott et al. 2021; Macfarlane 2021). This negates the archive's potential as a welcoming space to incubate political thinking and actions—a key concern within activist agendas, as we will discuss in our case study chapters. Occupy London activist Ludovica Rogers (2018) discussed how movement cultures can be fragmented and split, which makes memory work and archiving more difficult. Especially, we were told, when Occupy London members experienced a 'password war', with different factions within the movement changing the passwords to key accounts and locking others out. Collectively, we explored campaigns to save archives, collections, magazines, newsletters and pamphlets and engaged in the mapping of memories of movements. We also explored the protesting of method itself, and shared ways of intervening in debates, creating temporary communities and generating data in novel ways.

What emerged from the network was that attending and caring for protest memories was risky business. It required institutional and practitioner reflexivity. The dilemmas for cultural institutions being actively

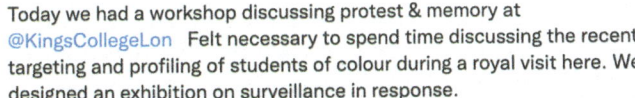

← **Protest Memory Network**
780 Tweets

Follow

⇄ **Protest Memory Network Retweeted**

Paula Serafini @lokitsch · 28 Mar 2019   · · ·

Today we had a workshop discussing protest & memory at
@KingsCollegeLon Felt necessary to spend time discussing the recent
targeting and profiling of students of colour during a royal visit here. We
designed an exhibition on surveillance in response.

KCL UCU is ready to escalate! and KCLSU

ılıl   💬 1   ⇄ 2   ♡ 7   ⬆

Fig. 1.2 Tweet of an exhibition proposal on surveillance and racist profiling in higher education.[8] Courtesy of Paula Serafini

involved in curating and supporting social justice movement work were captured by a curator from a large museum who noted that their institution was commonly a site of protest. This museum is very protective of their brand, we were told, which already compromised the kinds of relationships that could be developed with activists. Similarly, during our network engagements, an archivist raised the important question of "what is beyond the pale to remember?" They queried: what tactics or causes should be excluded? What is distasteful and anxiety-producing? While this book focuses on progressive social justice movements, a sister companion could certainly be produced on how to remember sensitively and informatively far-right, populist, nationalist, anti-LGBTIQ+ and racist protest cultures. In addition, more could be said from a memory perspective about the forms of exclusions that occur within progressive social movements, and the exclusions of protest memory between generations of activists.

A concrete outcome of the *Afterlives of Protest Research Network* was that activist memories needed to be newly theorised for the age of protest in connection with cultural institutions—in all their messy multiplicities, potentials and tensions.[9] As a mediated practice, cultural memory has the ability to do things in the world: to survey and support struggles for social justice; to bolster and participate in activist work; to commit to transformative organisational and cultural change; and to become a target of governmental, public and administrative ire. The protest of 'protest memory' therefore refers not only to how protest materials and subjects are approached and administered, but also to how a *protest memory ethos* can be generated within cultural institutions through a radical review of existing working practices and operations. To think in this way leads to the provocation: how can the operations of museums and archives be protested, challenged and opened up through activist-aligned memory work and knowledge?

ACTIVISM AND THE CULTURAL SECTOR

This short yet ambitious book focuses on the contemporary moment and locates our sustained empirical analysis within one national context: the United Kingdom. We engage with qualitative methods and approaches to protest memory collection, curation and activation, via the experiences of archivists, curators and activist practitioners and donors based in the UK, and against the backdrop of relevant practices and projects in the international museum and archive community. We limit our case study analysis to movements in which we have been active researchers and participants within: the feminist movement and the environmental movement. These movements share resonances in terms of their denouncements of wider power structures and both have seen renewals before, during and after the Covid-19 pandemic. In terms of material cultures, both produce materials and approaches that can 'sit within' mainstream heritage institutions in different ways. In presenting our empirical case studies, we connect our critical understanding of 'protest memory' with on-the-ground practitioner and activist research interviews, expert workshops and case study analysis of the museums and archives that worked closely with us in the network.

However, it is important to recognise that while this book is empirically grounded in the protest memory work surrounding contemporary feminist activist and environmental struggles, the spirit of this book is informed by the wider impact and legacies of the Black Lives Matter movement.[10] In 2020, George Floyd's digitally witnessed and virally remediated murder in Minneapolis, Minnesota at the hands of white police officer, Derek Chauvin, instigated the largest racial justice protests in the US since the civil rights movement, and since the anti-slavery abolition movement in the UK; this police killing being one injustice in a long line of police murders of Black men and women. As has been well documented, during the 2020 summer of unrest, BLM activists engaged in collective acts of de-commemoration and dissent against racist public memory cultures, including toppling and defacing statues to slave traders and owners (Burch-Brown 2020). These direct actions prompted cultural institutions (and corporations) to position themselves publicly: to issue statements of solidarity and to reflect upon issues of racial injustice and systematic inequities within their own organisations and to pledge change. This resulted in increased diversity initiatives (Dafoe and Goldstein 2020; Young 2021) and gave additional resonance to hashtag campaigns such as #OscarsSoWhite.

It also prompted a cultural conversation about 'performative allyship' (Kalina 2020), as museums and cultural institutions navigated the politics of public anti-racist statements, including the Instagram initiative of 'Black Out' squares. Many cultural institutions fell short on these speech acts, with numerous organisations facing a public backlash on social media for their silence, their performative allyship and/or their abysmal records of racial diversity and leadership within their workforces. This led to cultural institutions across the US and UK taking to their social media accounts to issue public apologies, stating a desire to 'do better' and to express public commitments to increasing diversity within the cultural sector (Greenberger and Solomon 2020). Such was the scrutiny placed on the cultural sector following renewed BLM protests, that ArtReview named Black Lives Matter the most influential actor in the artworld in 2020. The BLM movement was recognised in this top position on their annual Power 100 list for statue toppling, raising the visibility of Black artists and making museums rethink their role in society.

Within the UK context, the BLM impact should be viewed in tandem with initiatives to decolonise the past and to call into scrutiny colonial and slavery residues within the cultural sector, not least within museums. Attention given to such an agenda has met with governmental and right-wing backlash. Following the upsurge in BLM protests, the Culture Secretary Oliver Dowden overstepped governmental reach by announcing to museums and funding bodies: "The government does not support the removal of statues or other similar objects...You should not be taking actions motivated by activism or politics" (Hicks 2020).[11] In what has been deemed the UK's culture war, academic and heritage workers have been subjected to trolling and hostilities by 'anti-woke' politicians, newspaper editorials and mobilised publics following a report by the National Trust which documented connections with historic slavery in over 90 properties under their care (Huxtable et al. 2020). During a debate in the House of Commons on decolonising education curricula, the women and equalities minister, Kemi Badenoch, stated that schools would be breaking the law if they discussed white privilege and critical race theory, or showed support to "the anti-capitalist Black Lives Matter group", as she dismissed decolonising initiatives as a fad and one-sided bias (Murray 2020). A campaign to discredit anti-racism was further evident in the 2021 Sewell report, commissioned by the UK government in the wake of the BLM protests and intended to investigate racial discrimination in education, healthcare, work and policing.[12] The Sewell report declared that the UK had no significant problems of institutional racism, prompting an avalanche of criticism and public debate surrounding the methods, veracity and purpose of the report, which many deemed to "whitewash the problems of racism in Britain" (Bhopal 2021).

Taken together, we see a complex picture emerge in which activists, academics, politicians, heritage and cultural workers, educators and the general public are positioned within a heightened moment of activism, backlash and governmentality. The BLM movement has been instrumental in galvanising public opinion and forcing the hand of cultural institutions to demonstrate solidarity, reflexivity and a commitment to social justice change; to which the right-wing press, mobilised publics and the UK administration seeks to refute the 'woke' agenda and reinscribe the status quo and its structural amnesia. A similar backlash has been witnessed against climate emergency campaigners who target the cultural sector (Mance 2022). Accumulatively, this current conjuncture is one thick with tension around how protests past, present and future are to be institutionally understood and acted on (or stamped out). Cultural institutions must manoeuvre between demands for accountability and leadership, an impetus to document and engage in social activism as keepers of memory and history, and to position themselves carefully as public institutions, especially as charities or recipients of public funding which can create limitations on what projects are pursued, and in what ways. What is clear, however, is that this contemporary protest boom is accompanied with a new protest memory boom that requires careful navigation, ethical awareness and institutional self-reflexivity.

Museums and archives, as crucial sites of cultural memory production and contestation, have an important role to play in developing protest knowledge as a form of civic memory and literacy; to not only understand past-present-future protest as key to democratic engagement but also to understand how protest cultures can generate important cultural assets and signposts to future change. After all, archives provide "the tools or building-blocks upon which memory is constructed, framed, verified and ultimately accepted" (Flinn et al. 2009, p. 76). Similarly, museums "mediate the past, present and future and can be used to shape collective memory into official versions of the past. This process involves choices about what is remembered and what is forgotten; what is collected or preserved and presented, and what is not", as museums "are given a power in the memory-making processes to affirm and validate certain cultural expressions and interpretations" (Davison 2004, p. 202).[13] We contend that museums and archives can no longer afford to disengage with protest heritage, but at the same time, further guidance is needed. Indicatively, instructive guidance has been provided by the Black Lives Matter Charter for the UK Heritage Sector, produced collaboratively via the arts and education charity Culture& (2020). This charter sets out concrete actions in which cultural institutions can engage in racial justice work (Table 1.1). The aim of our book is to contribute to broader conversations on protest heritage and to provide further reflections on how cultural institutions can engage with contemporary protest cultures, navigate ethical sticking points, and how to position themselves within this broader 'activist turn' that demands a cultural commons of social justice and civic-based social change recognition.

Table 1.1 Excerpts from the Black Lives Matter Charter for the UK Heritage Sector, Culture& (2020)

Black Lives Matter Charter for the UK Heritage Sector
• The statements of horror about the killing of George Floyd in the US must be followed up by similar statements of support to the UK Black communities in relation to Black people who have died in similar circumstances in Britain
• Support decolonising collections [...] the imperial narratives around objects in museum collections that have supported or have been acquired by means of colonial aggression or with the profits of the transatlantic slave trade, must be identified as such, giving clear and explicit information to audiences on the history of the object and its acquisition, and how it came into the possession of the museum, investigating the reasons and deeper context
• Museums must make a commitment to the editing and rewording of racist artwork titles that include racially sensitive words or [...] descriptions of Black people which are considered outdated in the present day
• Where collections or objects have been acquired by force or other means without consent, museums must start the process of restitution and repatriation to their rightful owners, and where museums have profited from the ownership and display of cultural property, they must make proportionate funds available to set up relationships of exchange and cooperation
• Arts and heritage organisations must be publicly accountable via their funders such as Race Equality Action Plans, Arts Council England and DCMS targets for their actions in relation to tackling institutional racism and decolonising their workforce by taking steps to deal with subconscious bias and ensure that staff at all levels are representative of the diversity of the UK population
• Arts and heritage organisations must devise programmes that appeal to Black people in our society by commissioning and supporting diverse contemporary curators and artists to make alternative interpretations to address the history and present-day issues around racism, prejudice and social exclusion
• Arts and heritage organisations must take steps to holistically protect the mental health, wellbeing, and lives of their Black workforce in relation to navigating and challenging racism, and acknowledging stress and trauma where it has occurred

CONCEPTUALISING PROTEST MEMORY IN THE CULTURAL SECTOR

We approach 'protest memory' in three interconnected ways in this book; as theme, method and ethos. First, in its foundation, 'protest memory' refers to the personal, collective and cultural remembrance of past and present social movements and acts of protest. This remembrance is contoured through the institutional domains of museums and archives, which facilitate (or hinder) the generation of publicly accessible cultural memories of protest. Protest memory can thus be seen as a 'theme' or 'content' that is mediated via cultural institutions. Second, following from the specificities of protest cultures, as we will discuss in Chapter 2, protest memory can also be understood as a 'method' or 'form' of remembering. This aspect asks cultural institutions to reflexively question the curatorial techniques they use to remediate and remember protest; and, ultimately, to encourage and foreground democratic, civic and vernacular memory techniques (through, for example, co-creation and co-curation), alongside, or in place of, centring the official 'expert' narratives of the cultural institution. Third, we expand the analytical parameters of what can be termed 'protest memory' to draw much-needed attention to the forms of mnemonic labour and institutional practices that happen behind the scenes and how they can be analysed as an institutional 'ethos'. This aspect aims to map such practices against a rapidly evolving sector in which cultural institutions are both increasingly becoming targets of protest grievances, and are subject to emerging societal expectations that they should lend their symbolic power to represent and advocate on behalf of social justice struggles.

In short, the cultural sector is in a period of reckoning. By necessity, to engage in protest memory collection and curation is becoming a more profound and engaged undertaking, which can call into question the very working practices, values and standpoints of cultural institutions more widely. Increasingly, cultural institutions are using memory artefacts and techniques to encourage audiences to engage in forms of civic-based protest actions themselves, or to reflect on their capacities to do so. Cultural institutions are also being targeted by protesters—which in turn, generate pledges and statements, which must be remembered in order to track accountability (which we refer, in Chapter 6, as 'holistic accountability'). Protest memory, then, in our articulation, is more complex and implicated than the simple representational acts of collecting and exhibiting protest artefacts: there are cultural techniques and an underpinning protest memory ethos at play that calls into question the leadership, governance and social role of museums and archives as potential allies and actors in social justice actions.

It should be noted that when conceptualising our analytical framework within the *Afterlives of Protest Research Network*, academic participants queried our use of the term 'protest memory' on two counts. To begin, that people may have different understandings of protest. Then, that the term 'protest memory' may be adequately covered by terms already in circulation such as 'social movement memory'. Our book is a response to this from the nuanced perspective of working closely with museums, archives and activists who are experiencing unevenly distributed demands for engaging with protest memory. These cultural and heritage workers would welcome literature drawn from interdisciplinary and interprofessional fields to outline current understandings of activist, protest and social movement memorialisation that speaks to the new social role of cultural institutions. Our evocation of 'protest memory' therefore serves as an umbrella term inclusive of collecting and curating around protest in the public sphere, wider activist and social movement engagements with mainstream museums, archives, galleries and libraries, and how cultural institutions position themselves in terms of current activist campaigns and societal issues. We have elected to use 'protest memory' rather than social movement memory in recognition of the changing ways in which contention takes place, and to explore how museums and archives make sense (or not) of protest in its diverse forms and their own implications within these demands.

To contextualise, recent decades have seen the greater involvement of ordinary citizens in public contentions. This era has been named an "age of global mass protest" (Stirling Haig et al. 2020), in which protest in the public sphere is happening more frequently now than in any other historical period. Sociologists characterise this as a move away from the "normalisation of protest" to the "normalisation of the protester" (Van Aelst and Walgrave 2001, p. 461). We deem that the term 'protest' is potentially more expansive (but also more personalised) than 'social movements', as it resonates with the heightened cultural moment of protest which includes everyday citizens as well as movement actors.[14] Furthermore, the term 'protest memory' carries with it a sense of urgency and reckoning, particularly as museums and archives are increasingly becoming sites of protest attention, as we will explore. Such memory work should not be isolated or made temporary (as part of a 'trend' or as outsourced to temporary curators and exhibition projects) but should be deep, thoughtful and contextualised. This work can be placed in dialogue with the wider values and operating practices of the GLAM sector.

We argue that archives and museums are well placed to participate in this complex memory work due to their organisational remit to protect historical artefacts, to be socially relevant to diverse communities and visitors, to inspire critical thinking and to act as dialogic and civic spaces (Cameron and Kelly 2010; Fristrup 2019; Simon 2016; Watson 2007). Accordingly, we propose that cultural institutions can serve diverse communities and users best when they operate as productive sites of interaction: between *history* (conceptualised here as the events of the past and the selective evidentiary record and narrative of those events) and *memory* (which we articulate as the connective cultural work linking past, present and future subjectivities, imaginaries, values and actions). Museums and archives must consider their potential to do this work, regardless of their collections or scope. Indeed, protest memory does not just belong in art galleries or history museums and archives. What can protest memory bring to children's museums, science centres and wider heritage and ecological sites? At the same time, any invitation to engage in protest cultures necessitates a reflexive grappling with institutional legacies surrounding cultural, symbolic and physical violence. This includes cultural and heritage institutions being rooted, and complicit, in the knowledge structures and practices of white supremacy, ableism and heteropatriarchy (Giblin et al. 2019; Sullivan and Middleton 2020; Sandell and Nightingale 2012). To navigate across protest histories and memories effectively, we argue, cultural institutions may need to explore innovative methods of collaboration, representation, media convergence and pedagogical activism, including reflexivity over their forms of governance, policy, outreach and operating practices.

OVERVIEW OF CHAPTERS

This introductory chapter has set out the development of the *Afterlives of Protest Research Network* and our multi-modal approach to research collaboration and empirical research. In this chapter we have issued a flexible, heuristic conceptualisation of 'protest memory' as a theme and method of civic memory, and have set out our intention to explore the principles of an underpinning 'protest memory ethos' within the cultural sector. The remainder of this book will provide the theoretical, applied and evidential steps of our research in the UK national context, placed into wider conversation with transnational debates and examples.

Chapter 2 *Museums, Archives and Protest Memory* presents a critical synthesis of literature drawn from cultural memory studies, social movement studies, media and cultural studies and museum, archive and curatorial studies to delineate what we call a 'media-memory-activism nexus' through which protest memory projects take place in the cultural sector. We discuss the role of objects, material culture, mediation and visual culture within activist and social movement memory production.

This contributes to our framing of institutional remediations of protest memory as 'cultural techniques' (Siegert 2013) that seek to establish the chains of operations between humans, things and media. To achieve the interdisciplinary and interprofessional aims of the book, we further call for the need to think beyond entrenched disciplinary thinking that can cohere around concepts such as 'archival activism', 'museum activism' and 'memory activism' (see Flinn 2011; Janes and Sandell 2019; Gutman and Wüstenberg 2023) and begin to map important synergies and frictions between these ideas and practices.

Chapter 3 *Towards a Protest Memory Framework* provides an analytical lens for understanding the creation and securitisation of protest memory, grounded within practitioner-based examples and projects. Here we discuss five axes of protest memory produced within the GLAM sector, as identified within our empirical research and network activities. As part of our contribution towards a protest memory framework that thinks in close connection with the cultural sector, we identify museums and archives as (i) sites of protest, (ii) agents of protest, (iii) domains of protest memory, (iv) co-creators of protest memory and (v) protectors, carers and innovators of protest memory. We position protest memory as an ethos and practice that imbricates institutional frameworks and assembles heritage professionals, audiences, artists, activists, academics, citizens, media makers, technologies, material objects and immaterial assets. This framework is productive, creative and collaborative. Within it, we take a closer look at the creation and administration of protest memory within different modes of power sharing, including the contemporary agenda of co-creation and co-production, and how this has been pursued with a focus on activism and protest.

Chapter 4 *Rapid Response Collecting* provides the first empirical case study. Centring on the transnational Women's March which marked the first day in office of contentious US President Donald Trump (2017–2021), this case study examines the role of contemporary, cause-based collecting in museums and archives. Analysing news sources, social media data and in-depth expert interviews with curators, archivists, collections and public engagement staff at the Bishopsgate Institute (London), People's History Museum (Manchester) and Victoria and Albert Museum (London), this chapter examines the institutional processes behind collecting and curatorial efforts, including the important role of social media. We examine the cultural value these case study institutions deemed the protests to hold, what material culture was collected and how the

Women's March was put into dialogue with historic protest to generate new protest memories. Through the example of the Women's March, we demonstrate not only the sped-up commemorative and documentary rhythms of contemporary protest cultures, but also how memory is conceived prospectively, rather than as pertaining to after the event. Furthermore, we draw attention to the presence (and lack) of intersectionality in the archive and assess public debates surrounding contemporary collecting of activist cultures. Finally, we explore how museum and archive professionals navigate memory work and their understanding of institutional (memory) activism.

Chapter 5 *Activist Memory and the Archive* provides case study two and explores the sustainability of climate protest memory within the wider context of research on water and memory, focusing on the activist arts organisation Platform (1983–present). The chapter argues that a climate of protest memory is not a trend but rather is wrought from and depends upon archives, museums, media and artists to continually renew their approaches to co-production with audiences, engagement with educators and local communities. Platform offers a unique case study that is connected internationally to a growing campaign around urban environments, inclusive civic participation and engaged citizens, working with cultural and media organisations to create sustained and new approaches to remembering environmental protest. It is their multidirectional approach to archiving their London river activist work from 1992 to the present, working closely with the Bishopsgate Institute (London), that sheds light on the memory work required to sustain environmental activism.

Chapter 6 *Reflections on Precarity and Risk* concludes the book and summarises protest memory as a multidirectional commitment. This commitment spans the collections and resources that institutions acquire and showcase, but it is also an ethos, value statement and orientation that shines a light on the wider work the collecting-archiving-curatorial institution is doing to uphold social justice values and to make their institutions accessible and accountable to diverse publics and communities of interest. This is risky work. In the context of funding challenges, culture wars and a cascade of social and health vulnerabilities affecting all aspects of cultural and creative work, to engage with protest memory takes courage and dedication. In its expression and curation, a *protest memory ethos* both challenges and innovates the operational work of museums and archives on the ground. To conclude we offer a series of reflections from the *Afterlives of Protest Research Network* to help guide future practice. As we suggest, protest materials, and the human agents who create them, are rich with meaning, potency and declarations of past lives and future prospects. Their innovative potential calls for articulation, contextualisation and a culture of care.

NOTES

1. In *Media and Memory*, Garde-Hansen (2011, pp. 18–29) sketches three phases of memory studies which may be useful for readers unfamiliar with developments in this field. The first phase spans the late nineteenth and early twentieth centuries and incorporates the foundational thinking of Halbwachs, Bartlett, Bergson and Warburg. These thinkers demonstrate how memory, even personal memory, is not individual but is social and relational; memory is embodied, habitual and creative. The second phase sees the emergence of memory studies as a discipline, from the 1980s onwards. Key thinkers include Lowenthal, Connerton, Nora, Huyssen, Jan and Aleida Assmann. This work tackles issues of history versus memory, heritage, museums, trauma, remembering, forgetting, amnesia, archives, memorials and nostalgia. The third phase, from the new millennium, provides a greater focus on the production of memory through media technologies, including digital media, and the role of memory as mobile and malleable in transnational, cosmopolitan and postcolonial contexts. Key thinkers include Erll, Hoskins, Rigney, Reading, Rothberg and van Dijck. Memory scholars are now calling for a fourth wave of memory studies, pushing the field to go beyond the anthropocentric to think ecologically, as well as to centre a concern with activism and human resistance and agency.

2. While this chapter signposts contemporary protest archive collections, it should be noted that the value of protest has long been recognised by community and institutional archives around the globe. Numerous institutions hold historic collections of activist materials and records from trade unions, student campaigning groups, liberation and revolutionary, social justice and civil rights movements. Such collections provide key documentary evidence of social change and the struggles to achieve it, preserved for research and posterity. For example, this ethos is at play in the International

Institute of Social History in Amsterdam, which has been collecting social movement records since the 1920s. This archive is dedicated to "preserving the heritage of often oppressed social movements" in pursuit of enhancing "the quality of the world's memory" and contributing "to a vibrant civil society". This mission statement resonates with our framing of protest memory as civic memory (https://iisg.amsterdam/en/about/mission).

3. This activist and social justice drive is evidenced in the launch of the Activist Museum Award (https://le.ac.uk/rcmg/research-arc hive/activist-museum-award) and the rise of professional networks instigated by heritage workers of colour such as Museums Detox, Archives Download, We Are Transmission and Intersectional GLAM (Chilcott et al. 2021). Within the International Council of Museums (ICOM), there was an attempt in recent years to redefine 'the museum' to embrace a social justice dimension. This was debated yet ultimately rejected for being too political and was replaced with a progressive, yet less transformative definition for policy purposes (see Etges and Dean 2022).

4. The formation of the *Afterlives of Protest Research Network* (AoP) was inspired by a local university Occupy movement. During 2013, students at the University of Warwick returned to the hallowed ground of mass protest at the university, Senate House, which in 1975 had seen significant unrest. The university administration had moved its seat of power to another part of the campus, but student occupiers targeted a building with a *protest-sense-of-place-memory*. The re-materialisation of protest memory by a new generation generated the research questions underpinning the network. Once a protest has been cleared away, the tables and chairs back in place, the streets cleaned and the walls re-painted, *where is protest memory, where does it go, who has it and how can we access it?* Museums and archives along with activists and protesters are key players in helping researchers answer these questions.

5. The AoP logo drew on general protest aesthetics (a background simulating the texture of cardboard that speaks to protest signs; a megaphone; a fist raised in solidarity; an image of riot police), alongside more specific protest iconography. This includes the international feminist symbol and the Guy Fawkes inspired mask, the latter associated with protest from the Occupy movement and

the hacktivist collective Anonymous. Notably, the mask iconography was reappropriated by protesters from the work of illustrator David Lloyd and the 1980s comic strip *V for Vendetta*. It provides a good example of how cultural memory and protest collide through acts of remediation (the reuse of previous media content in new contexts). The Cartoon Museum in London held a *V for Vendetta: Behind the Mask* exhibition in 2021, detailing the origins of the mask and how its iconography travelled through graphic novels and the blockbuster movie adaptation *V for Vendetta* (McTeigue, dir. 2005) to become a popular protest icon for a range of contemporary causes. This example details how the media-memory-activism nexus coalesces, which we explore further in Chapter 2.

6. On 16 August 1819, armed cavalry attacked a peaceful mass rally of 60,000 men, women and children assembled in Manchester for parliamentary reform and anti-poverty measures. The event became known as The Peterloo Massacre. An estimated 18 people died from sabre cuts and trampling. Nearly 700 received serious injuries. The Peterloo Massacre is considered a defining moment in Britain's democratic history, paving the way for working class men to win the right to vote. PHM's exhibition *Disrupt? Peterloo and Protest* took place between 23 March 2019 and 23 February 2020 (https://phm.org.uk/exhibitions/disrupt-peterloo-and-protest).

7. The first museum of British LGBTIQ+ history and culture, *Queer Britain*, opened in King's Cross, London in 2022, in advance of the 50th anniversary of the UK's first gay pride march. Prior to gaining its own location, Queer Britain staged temporary exhibitions. Its exhibition *We Are Queer Britain* won Best Small Museum Project 2022, awarded by the Museums Association as part of their Museums Change Lives campaign. When not on display, the museum's collection is housed at the Bishopsgate Institute (https://queerbritain.org.uk).

8. This exhibition proposal was presented at the Curating Protest Memory workshop by network participants. It drew attention to a recent event at the workshop's host university, King's College London, where activist students of colour—the majority of whom were Muslim—were barred from entering university premises during a Royal visit to attend their classes (Adams 2019). The students were targeted for being members of student political organisations including Justice for Cleaners and Action Palestine.

The arts-based exhibition proposal centred on a teach-out at the university highlighting racist surveillance practices within higher education. The exhibition proposers made use of the miniature plastic surveillance cameras that came with the museum toy kit, a staff ID, and, in a powerful use of 'digital memory' (Hoskins 2018), mobile phone footage of the sound of student ID cards being refused entry.

9. There are many forms of activist, protest and social movement memory that require investigation if we are to understand (comparatively and critically) how audiences, publics and communities engage with social justice in the present. Pertinent examples include the *ReAct: Remembering Activism* project funded by the European Research Council (https://rememberingactivism.eu), the *Remembering and Forgetting: Media, Memory, Activism* project funded by the Leverhulme Foundation (www.protestmemory.com), *Black Lives Matter: Usable Pasts and International Futures*, funded by UK Research and Innovation (https://gtr.ukri.org/projects?ref=AH%2FP007066%2F1) and *Protests, Art Practices and Culture of Memory in the post-Yugoslav context*, funded by the Slovenian Research Agency (www.ff.uni-lj.si/en/protests-art-practices-and-culture-memory-post-yugoslav-context).

10. Black Lives Matter (BLM) is an international activist movement that campaigns and protests white supremacist violence and systemic racism towards Black people. BLM was launched in 2013 as a hashtag and then as a series of local chapters and decentralised protest actions, with three Black women and radical community organisers as the movement's instigators: Alicia Garza, Patrisse Cullors and Opal Tometi (https://blacklivesmatter.com).

11. The UK government has a 'retain and explain' policy for contentious heritage assets (including public memorials, statues, monuments and commemorations) which face public calls for removal. The 2023 policy outlines that such assets should be kept in place, accompanied by an explanation of their historical context; if removal is deemed necessary a planning application must be submitted. Notably, following BLM and anti-racist topplings of statues, the government has now issued statues legal protection (https://www.gov.uk/government/news/retain-and-explain-guidance-published-to-protect-historic-statues).

12. The Sewell report is available at: https://assets.publishing.ser vice.gov.uk/media/6062ddb1d3bf7f5ce1060aa4/20210331_-_ CRED_Report_-_FINAL_-_Web_Accessible.pdf.

13. Historical research has previously articulated the domains of 'official memory' construction (such as museums, archives, political speeches, commemorative rituals and public memorials, produced by elites to advance particular national narratives and agendas which uphold institutional power and the status quo) and 'vernacular memory' (the heterogeneous, embodied, everyday experiences of 'ordinary people' which provide micro-narratives, including of dissent and resistance) (see Bodnar 1991). This book explores the intersection of official memory and civic memory practices through the lens of contemporary protest cultures and their presence within, and contestations of, cultural institutions.

14. Famously, *Time* magazine named 'The Protestor' as their person of the year in 2011 (Andersen 2011). While invoking 'protest' in our concept 'protest memory', we note that this nomenclature may fail to resonate with various communities and that, equally, such terms may hold localised meanings. First Nations and indigenous actors in the realm of environmental justice, for example, might perceive their role as more akin to water and land custodians—and defenders—than as protesters (Robertson 2019). In the Arab world, an activist (*nashit* in Arabic) is someone closely associated with the leftist political parties most active from the 1950s to the 1970s; *nishat* (activism) refers to forms of political resistance explicitly juxtaposed to party politics, social movements and civil society organisations, so that activism is understood more widely as non-institutionalised form of resistance (Schwedler and Harris 2016). Like Schwedler and Harris, we argue that the vocabularies of activism and protest vary across time and space, and the goal is "not to fix the meanings of those terms, but to appreciate the politics that the lexicons of activists reveal" (2016, p. 3). Likewise, it is instructive to chart which vocabularies museums and archives deploy to speak of cultures of resistance, and which terms they align with their own institutional work on issues of social inequities and injustices.

References

Adams, R. 2019. University Barred 10 Students from Campus During Queen's Visit. *Guardian*, March 22. Available: www.theguardian.com/education/2019/mar/22/kings-college-london-barred-10-students-from-campus-during-queens-visit. Accessed 9 Oct 2022.

Andersen, K. 2011. The Protester. *Time*, December 14. Available: http://content.time.com/time/specials/packages/article/0,28804,2101745_2102132_2102373,00.html. Accessed 9 Oct 2022.

Arness-Dalton, D. 2019. Roundtable Talk. Future Directions—Activist Museums Panel. *Curating Protest Memory Expert Workshop*, March 28. King's College London.

ArtReview. 2020. Power 100. Available: https://artreview.com/power-100?year=2020. Accessed 9 Oct 2022.

Bhopal, K. 2021. The Sewell Report Displays a Basic Misunderstanding of How Racism Works. *Guardian*, March 31. Available: https://www.theguardian.com/commentisfree/2021/mar/31/sewell-report-racism-government-racial-disparity-uk. Accessed 9 Oct 2022.

Bodnar, J. 1991. *Remaking America: Public Memory, Commemoration and Patriotism in the Twentieth Century*. Princeton: Princeton University Press.

Burch-Brown, J. 2020. Should Slavery's Statues Be Preserved? On Transitional Justice and Contested Heritage. *Journal of Applied Philosophy* 39 (5): 807–824.

Butler, S.R., and E. Lehrer, eds. 2016. *Curatorial Dreams: Critics Imagine Exhibitions*. Montreal: McGill-Queen's University Press.

Cameron, F., and L. Kelly, eds. 2010. *Hot Topics, Public Culture, Museums*. Newcastle upon Tyne: Cambridge Scholars.

Caswell, M. 2021. *Urgent Archives: Enacting Liberatory Memory Work*. New York: Routledge.

Chidgey, R. 2018. *Feminist Afterlives: Assemblage Memory in Activist Times*. Cham: Palgrave Macmillan.

Chilcott, A., K. Fife, J. Lowry, J. Moran, A. Oke, A. Sexton, and J. Thethi. 2021. Against Whitewashing: The Recent History of Anti-Racist Action in the British Archives Sector. *The International Journal of Information, Diversity, & Inclusion* 5 (1): 33–59.

Chynoweth, A., B. Lynch, K. Petersen, and S. Smed, eds. 2020. *Museums and Social Change: Challenging the Unhelpful Museum*. London: Routledge.

Culture&. 2020. Black Lives Matter Charter for the UK Heritage Sector. Available: https://www.cultureand.org/news/black-lives-matter-charter-for-the-uk-heritage-sector. Accessed 9 Oct 2022.

Dafoe, T., and C. Goldstein. 2020. The George Floyd Protests Spurred Museums to Promise Change: Here's What They've Actually Done So Far. *ArtNet*,

August 14. Available: https://news.artnet.com/art-world/museums-divers ity-equity-commitments-1901564. Accessed 9 Oct 2022.

Davison, P. 2004. Museums and the Re-shaping of Memory. In *Heritage, Museums and Galleries*, ed. G. Corsane, 184–194. London: Routledge.

Della Ratta, D., K. Dickinson, and S. Haugbolle, eds. 2020. *The Arab Archives: Mediated Memories and Digital Flows*. Amsterdam: Institute of Network Cultures.

Erde, J. 2014. Constructing Archives of the Occupy Movement. *Archives and Records* 35 (2): 77–92.

Etges, A., and D. Dean. 2022. Definition Under Debate: What Makes a Museum? *De Gruyter Conversations*, August 11. Available: https://blog.deg ruyter.com/definition-under-debate-what-makes-a-museum. Accessed 9 Oct 2022.

Flinn, A. 2011. Archival Activism: Independent and Community-Led Archives, Radical Public History and the Heritage Professions. *InterActions: UCLA Journal of Education and Information Studies* 7: 2. Available: https://doi. org/10.5070/D472000699. Accessed 9 Oct 2022.

Flinn, A., M. Stevens, and E. Shepherd. 2009. Whose Memories, Whose archives?: Independent Community Archives, Autonomy, and the Mainstream. *Archival Science* 9 (1–2): 71–86.

Francis, S. 2019. Roundtable Talk, with Jane Trowell: Future Directions— Activist Museums Panel. *Curating Protest Memory Expert Workshop*, March 28. King's College London.

Fristrup, T., ed. 2019. *Socially Engaged Practices in Museums and Archives*. Östersund: Jam,li Forlag.

Garde-Hansen, J. 2011. *Media and Memory*. Edinburgh: Edinburgh University Press.

Giblin, J., I. Ramos, and N. Grout. 2019. Dismantling the Master's House: Thoughts on Representing Empire and Decolonising Museums and Public Spaces in Practice. *Third Text* 33 (4–5): 471–486.

Gledhill, J. 2012. Collecting Occupy London: Public Collecting Institutions and Social Protest Movements in the 21st Century. *Social Movement Studies* 11 (3–4): 342–348.

Greenberger, A., and T. Solomon. 2020. Major US Museums Criticized for Responses to Ongoing George Floyd Protests. *ArtNews*, June 2. Available: https://www.artnews.com/art-news/news/museums-controversy-george-floyd-protests-1202689494. Accessed 9 Oct 2022.

Gutman, Y. 2019. Keynote—The Cultural Mediation of Collective Action: Nakba Tours and Testimonies in Israel. 9 September. *The Afterlives of Protest Conference*. People's History Museum, Manchester.

Gutman, Y., and J. Wüstenberg, eds. 2023. *The Routledge Companion of Memory Activism*. New York: Routledge.

Hargreaves, I. 2016. Are You a Creative Citizen? In *The Creative Citizen Unbound: How Social Media and DIY Culture contribute to Democracy, Communities and the Creative Economy*, ed. I. Hargreaves and J. Hartley, 1–24. Bristol: Policy Press.

Hicks, D. 2020. The UK Government Is Trying to Draw Museums into a Fake Culture War. *Guardian*, October 15. Available: https://www.theguardian.com/commentisfree/2020/oct/15/the-uk-government-is-trying-to-draw-museums-into-a-fake-culture-war. Accessed 9 Oct 2022.

Hoskins, A., ed. 2018. *Digital Memory Studies: Media Pasts in Transition*. New York: Routledge.

Huxtable, S.-A., C. Fowler, C. Kefalas, and E. Slocombe. 2020. *Interim Report on the Connections Between Colonialism and Properties Now in the Care of the National Trust, Including Links with Historic Slavery*. Available: https://www.nationaltrust.org.uk/who-we-are/research/addressing-our-histories-of-colonialism-and-historic-slavery. Accessed 9 Oct 2022.

Janes, R.R., and R. Sandell, eds. 2019. *Museum Activism*. London: Routledge.

Jasper, J. 2018. *The Emotions of Protest*. Chicago: University of Chicago Press.

Kalina, P. 2020. Performative Allyship. *Technium Social Sciences Journal* 11: 478–481.

Macfarlane, K.S.M. 2021. How Do UK Archivists Perceive 'White Supremacy' in the UK Archives Sector? *Archives and Records* 42 (3): 266–283.

McTeigue, J. dir. 2005. *V for Vendetta*.

Mance, H. 2022. Can Just Stop Oil Make the Case for Protest? *Financial Times*, December 9. Available: https://www.ft.com/content/4a0ab6f3-83fc-4e89-b6a2-c05c85f3791b. Accessed 15 May 2023.

Message, K. 2014. *Museums and Social Activism: Engaged Protest*. New York: Routledge.

Message, K. 2018. *The Disobedient Museum: Writing at the Edge*. New York: Routledge.

Message, K. 2020. *Collecting Activism, Archiving Occupy Wall Street*. New York: Routledge.

Mills, E. 2016. Campaign for Museum of Gay History. *Museums Association*, November 23. Available: www.museumsassociation.org/museums-journal/news/2016/11/23112016-campaign-for-museum-of-gay-history. Accessed 9 Oct 2022.

Murawski, M. 2021. *Museums as Agents of Change: A Guide to Becoming a Changemaker*. Lanham: Rowman & Littlefield.

Murray, J. 2020. Teaching White Privilege as Uncontested Fact Is Illegal, Minister Says. *Guardian*, October 21. Available: https://www.theguardian.com/world/2020/oct/20/teaching-white-privilege-is-a-fact-breaks-the-law-minister-says. Accessed 9 Oct 2022.

Raicovich, L. 2021. *Culture Strike: Art and Museum in an Age of Protest.* London: Verso.

Ribeiro de Menezes, A., and C. Wong. 2018. Recipe for a Revolution: Empanadas and the Memories of Chilean Women Exiles in the UK. *Researching Protest Memory Expert Workshop,* May 30. University of Sussex.

Robertson, K. 2019. *Tear Gas Epiphanies: Protest, Culture, Museums.* Montreal: McGill-Queen's University Press.

Rogers, L. 2018. Roundtable Talk. Archiving Occupy: The Role of Activists, Museums and Academics in Preserving Social Movement Memory. *Circulating Protest Memory Expert Workshop,* September 17. Loughborough University.

Rollason-Cass, S., and S. Reed. 2015. Living Movements, Living Archives: Selecting and Archiving Web Content During Times of Social Unrest. *New Review of Information Networking* 20 (1–2): 241–247.

Ross, C. 2013. Occupy Collecting. *History Workshop Journal* 75 (1): 237–246.

Salahu-Din, D.T. 2019. Documenting the Black Lives Matter Movement in Baltimore through Contemporary Collecting: An Initiative of the National Museum of African American History and Culture. *Collections: A Journal for Museum and Archive Professionals* 15 (2–3): 101–112.

Sandell, R., and E. Nightingale, eds. 2012. *Museums, Equality and Social Justice.* London: Routledge.

Schwartz, G. 2019. Keynote—Icons of Justice and Playful Protest: Games and Occupations in Brazil. 9 September. *The Afterlives of Protest Conference.* People's History Museum, Manchester.

Schwedler, J., and K. Harris. 2016. What Is Activism? *Middle East Report* 281: 2–5.

Seremetakis, N., ed. 1994. *The Senses Still: Perception and Memory as Material Culture in Modernity.* Chicago: University of Chicago Press.

Siegert, B. 2013. Cultural Techniques: Or the End of the Intellectual Postwar Era in German Media Theory. *Theory, Culture & Society* 30 (6): 48–65.

Simon, N. 2016. *The Art of Relevance.* Santa Cruz: Museum 2.0. Available: http://www.artofrelevance.org. Accessed 9 Oct 2022.

Stirling Haig, C., Schmidt, K., and Brannen, S. 2020. The Age of Mass Protests: Understanding an Escalating Global Trend. *Center for Strategic and International Studies.* Available: https://www.csis.org/analysis/age-mass-protests-understanding-escalating-global-trend. Accessed 9 Oct 2022.

Sullivan, N., and C. Middleton. 2020. *Queering the Museum.* New York: Routledge.

Toonen, S. 2019. Remembering Activism Through Co-Creation: Protest Exhibitions. *Curating Protest Memory Expert Workshop,* March 28. King's College London.

Van Aelst, P., and S. Walgrave. 2001. Who Is That (Wo)man in the Street? From the Normalisation of Protest to the Normalisation of the Protester. *European Journal of Political Research* 39 (4): 461–486.
Watson, S., ed. 2007. *Museums and Their Communities*. New York: Routledge.
Young, C. 2021. Scotland's Response to George Floyd and Black Lives Matter: One Year On. *Coalition for Racial Equality and Rights*, May 25. Available: https://www.crer.org.uk/blog/george-floyd-one-year-on. Accessed 9 Oct 2022.

CHAPTER 2

Museums, Archives and Protest Memory

Abstract This chapter presents a critical synthesis of literature drawn from cultural memory studies, social movement studies, media and cultural studies and museum, archive and curatorial studies to further understand key issues surrounding protest, activism and social movements, and their connections to memory discourses and practices. With focused attention on the role of material culture, visual culture and remediation as 'cultural techniques' (Siegert 2013) within activist and social movement memory production, we introduce the 'media-memory-activism nexus' as an important analytic to understand how protest memory is produced and contested. To achieve the interdisciplinary and interprofessional aims of the book, we further call for the need to think beyond the entrenched disciplinary thinking that can cohere around concepts such as 'archival activism', 'museum activism' and 'memory activism' (see Flinn 2011; Janes and Sandell 2019; Gutman and Wüstenberg 2023) and begin to map important synergies and frictions between these ideas and practices.

Keywords Media-memory-activism nexus · Memory activism · Museum activism · Archival activism

R. Chidgey and J. Garde-Hansen, *Museums, Archives and Protest Memory*, Palgrave Macmillan Memory Studies, https://doi.org/10.1007/978-3-031-44478-4_2

INTRODUCTION

To help articulate the emerging connections between protest, memory, museums and archives, this chapter sets out the argument that memory and protest operate as *cultural techniques* within activist networks, and by extension, through contemporary museum and archive spaces. Taking the ideas of Bernhard Siegert (2013, pp. 48, 61) as emblematic of thinking in this area, cultural techniques refer to the "chains of operations that link humans, things, media", and which symbolically operationalise "distinctions in the real". We contend that these distinctions translate to the sum of administration, governance and creativity that underpins how protest, social movements and activism *come into* museums and archives, how they are categorised and what value they are perceived to have—which is then communicated back via the institution and beyond, internally and externally. We have italicised the phrase 'come into' here as an important matter of classification: what 'is' the museum or archive as an institution, as an "agent of change" (Murawski 2021), as a threshold of knowledge and as a site and source of protest memory are ongoing points of debate that we will seek to address.

Acting on Siegert's understanding of cultural techniques, we use this conceptualisation to propose a series of provocations that steer the discussions and case studies examined in this book. These provocations include: how do authoritative public museums and archives conceptualise and respond to protest, both historically and currently unfolding? What texts and practices do cultural institutions view as the materials of protest, how are such materials captured and curated and what decision-making processes underpin what is included, left out or discarded? How are protest materials repositioned within curatorial, archival, medial and administrative frameworks to reach new audiences and activist beneficiaries? In sum, how do cultural memory institutions manage both the risks and potential opportunities associated with 'live' protest heritage? To help address these queries, this chapter advances an understanding of protest memory as a cultural technique that can be cultivated by scholars and practitioners, but which is fraught with many difficulties.

UNDERSTANDING THE TERRAIN: PROTEST, ACTIVISM AND SOCIAL MOVEMENTS

Before we outline how protest memory can be viewed as a cultural technique in cultural institutions, it is worth clarifying our use of terms further. There are important distinctions to be made between protest, activism and social movements; an understanding of which can better serve memory workers in the heritage and cultural sector, alongside researchers and students more widely. While protest, activism and social movements are inevitably interlocking fields of practice, becoming sensitised to conceptual understandings of these terms can lead to useful reflections on the scope of institutional and academic practice within the field of memory and contentious actions—including what is being focused on, prioritised and left out.

Protest: In this book we deploy the term 'protest memory' as a flexible term, inclusive of remembering cultures and practices surrounding activism and social movements more widely. More specifically, protest refers to a series of events or acts that seek to challenge structural conditions deemed to be discriminatory, unjust or unethical—be they legal, cultural, social, economic or technological. The etymology of the term 'protest' comes from the Latin *prōtestārī*, "to bear witness together, to testify publicly" (Hirsch 2019, p. 16). Protest is intentional, frequently disruptive, and is mobilised to create wider public understandings of a grievance with the intention to voice dissent, to halt business as usual and to lead to alternative futures or outcomes. Protest can encompass the sole protester, such as Greta Thunberg's solitary action outside the Swedish parliament in 2018 in the name of climate action (which spurred international school strikes), to large-scale acts of disobedience including occupations of public squares and buildings, mass demonstrations and boycotts. Protest can be violent, including the destruction of property and life, and it can be non-violent (sit-ins, cabarets, blocking thoroughfares, street performance). In the new millennium, non-violent protesters increasingly target high-profile mediated events, such as the Olympic Games, televised sports and film premiers, and symbolically prestigious sites such as museums and art galleries. As a conditioning event to thinking about the construction and activation of protest memory through museums and archives, it is crucial to acknowledge that protest is increasingly happening through and against the cultural sector, with increased salience around issues of labour, representation, arts sponsorship, governance, racism and the climate emergency (see Coody Cooper 2008; Giannini 2019; Raicovich 2021; Robertson 2019). As we discuss further in Chapter 3, this has implications for how activism enters and engages with cultural memory institutions.

Activism: Our modern-day understanding of 'activism' finds its root in the Latin *actus*, which refers to *a doing and a driving force*. If we approach protest as event-based, and temporally and spatially bound, activism denotes a longer-term commitment and a diffuse set of actions. Activist sensibilities are required to compose campaigns, networks, countercultures and movements in order to materialise alternatives to the status quo. It should be noted that activism—like protest and social movements—occurs across the political spectrum. Activism can involve left-wing and progressive actions, or regressive and far-right articulations alike. Activist outputs include media and cultural productions; experiments with alternative economic systems, relationships and living arrangements; knowledge-building and consciousness-raising; community support and provision; and much more. Activism is not homogeneous and is rarely static. This is exemplified by Micah White (2016), co-founder of Occupy Wall Street, who recently heralded 'the end of protest'. He suggests that mass mobilisation in the public sphere is now safely contained and expected by governing powers in Western liberal democracies, therefore failing to create leverage for direct political change. White proposes that activists and protesters must innovate their tactics to achieve their goals. This encourages expanded definitions and practices of activism, such as 'cultural resistance' (Duncombe 2002), 'creative activism' (Harrebye 2016), 'art activism' (Serafini et al. 2018), 'consumer activism' (Lekakis 2022), 'digital activism' (Joyce 2010) and 'data activism' (Gutiérrez 2018). Each moniker brings forward the role of cultural production, performance, creativity, art, consumer culture, digital tools and data as sites of regulation and/or liberation to the fore. These understandings of the cultural and technical aspects of activism can be fruitful areas for further curatorial and collecting attention.

Social Movements: As defined by James Jasper, social movements are created by "conscious, concerted, and relatively sustained efforts by organized groups of ordinary people (as opposed to, say political parties, the military, or industrial trade groups) to change some aspect of their society by extrainstitutional means" (1997, p. 5). Jasper conceptualises four pivotal factors that scaffold the emergence, maintenance and collapse of social movements in the public sphere: resources, strategies, culture and biography. These factors are useful for heritage workers to take note of in terms of their collecting and curatorial efforts. *Resources* refer to the tools and technologies through which actors strive to make social change. *Strategies* refer to the choices, pathways and tactics mobilised, while *culture* refers to shared understandings as well as the cultural artefacts produced by activists. *Biography* refers to the individual psychic lives, social networks and lived experiences of human actors. A key element of social movement memory, then, is to grapple with the organisational elements of how collective and mass protest erupts: its conditioning factors, its strategies, its techniques, its successes and its failures. Protest memory caretakers can ask: What brings a person to a movement, what keeps them there, what do they do, what have been their struggles and joys and how do they understand the impact and legacy of their activist work? They can also ask: what new social imaginaries and daily practices are brought into being through social movement enterprise?

Thinking in tandem with Jasper's four dimensions of protest, we contend that social movements (and thus the conditions for social movement memory) have significantly shifted in their composition and execution in past decades. The bricks-and-mortar activist institutions of the early to late twentieth century—when many social movements had dedicated buildings to work in, printing presses, local chapters, even paid organisers and cultural workers—have given way to increasingly decentralised and precarious grassroots networks and coalitions. Today's networks are frequently choreographed via digital media both locally and transnationally, erupting in manifestly 'leaderless movements' (Castells 2015). This creates both challenges and possibilities for institutional protest memory caretakers. Today, much grassroots activism is coordinated via online means, resulting in born-digital and digitised collections of activist materials. As activist digital records are frequently held on proprietary social media sites, this provides key challenges for archivists and curators to acquire and accession on technological, legal and ethical grounds (Velte 2018; Della Ratta et al. 2020; Chidgey 2020; Tong 2022).[1]

BETWEEN THE FRAGILITY AND MEMORABILITY OF PROTEST: OBJECTS, IMAGES AND MATERIAL CULTURE

Social movements and media systems are inherently linked; this is the starting point for any approach to protest memory curation. As Graham Meikle (2018) contends, while there have always been crowds, uprisings and insurrections, social movements as a political mode of contention are a modern phenomenon, emerging at the same time as modern media systems:

> Anti-slavery abolitionists made use of newspaper ads, pamphlets, and the postal service; labour movements established their own newspapers. As photography and telegraphy, then telephony, radio, cinema, television and the internet emerged, social movements found ways to use these. Newsreel footage of Suffragettes can still shock, a century on; audio recording of Martin Luther King can still electrify and galvanize, half a century after his death; and shaky mobile phone footage of police violence shared across Facebook can turn disparate individuals into a collective voice. (Meikle 2018, p. 3)

Drawing on Meikle, we can reflect on how protest cultures are mediated and what connections and affects these forms of mediation have in the world. Protest media ranges from the amateur, hand-made, to the professionally produced, to the appropriation of existing media forms and platforms. Mediated by material culture, bodies and emotions, protest is also composed through affective states, which seek to give resonance and urgency to activist acts: whether this is to produce a state of anger, confusion, courage or joy, in which to create ripples and disruptions in society. When understanding protest cultures, it is likewise important to think beyond the protester or their singular media productions: within protest assemblages are wider contributors and witnesses, including police, security guards, soldiers, bystanders, journalists, academics, creative workers and citizens. Underpinning these agents and carriers of protest memories are the discursive frameworks derived from mainstream media and politicians, who represent these movements back to wider publics. Such media memory agents are instrumental in shaping understandings of who are the 'victim' and 'aggressor' within protest scenarios, how disruption, violence and justice are discursively framed and what is presented as the problem, the demands and the proposed solution of acts of collective grievance. Collectively, these objects, forms of mediation, affects and discourses constitute the assemblage of 'protest afterlives' (Chidgey 2018) that we consider in this book.

While music, performance, visual arts and activist print cultures have garnered the most scholarly attention to date, objects used for protest have so far been under-theorised. When objects appear in exhibitions on protest, more attention is paid to their aesthetic qualities rather than their production or use values. As Anna Feigenbaum explains, more than "background scenery or mere props for action", non-human objects such as protest signs, tents, megaphones and tear gas, "have their own stories to tell about how they mediate and communicate political struggle" (2014, p. 15). Objects operate as fundamental elements in wider protest assemblages, accruing not only use-value and object biographies, but becoming 'sticky' with emotions and feelings. They operate as mediators of action, imaginaries, affect and mnemonic consequence (Chidgey 2018; Flood and Grindon 2014).

Within this multi-media assemblage of protest memory, journalists and photojournalists have heightened roles to play in constructing public social imaginaries and afterlives of protest memories across time and space. These media workers create prevalent and accessible understandings of past and present social movements, providing the 'first draft of history', as well as its subsequent revisioning through commemorative reporting, the use of historical analogies and news organisations that remediate their institutional media archives in the digital age (Edy 1999; Hajek et al. 2016). Within the terrain of cultural and mediated memory, it is important to note that most protest is forgotten. The details, the names, the motivations and the actions are often lost to the historic record, or intentionally buried or ignored. This speaks to the "fragility of activism's histories" (Cvetkovich 2003, p. 231), and the significant recovery work that curators often face when representing protest legacies, and the opportunities to work with activists to do so.

When protest becomes 'memorable', and circulates within public imaginaries, this is the result of select actors and events having garnered considerable media attention, replayed across different media forms and time periods. Protest is therefore most often remembered in public imaginaries through high-intensity 'snap shots' of historical events that have garnered prolific media coverage and which travel in condensed visual images. We need to only think of the violent crackdown on pro-democracy protesters in 1989 in Tiananmen Square, Beijing, China, which is remembered around the world by the 'Tank Man' image of a lone protester standing courageously in front of a line of armoured tanks, captured by the American photojournalist Jeff Widener. As memory scholars have demonstrated, protest acts that involve some form of violence or threat of violence (carried out by protesters to property or done to protesters' bodies) often gain the most memory traction over generations (Rigney 2020). This resonates with research conducted with photojournalists, which establishes how these media workers respond to commercial expectations of what protest 'should look like', with the most lucrative protest imagery depicting violence or conflict (Veneti 2017).[2]

Indeed, complex systems of visibility, legibility and memorability are in operation with regard to how protest is designed by activists, framed by journalists and re-deployed visually within cultural and media environments, including in future protest movements (Rigney and Smits 2023). At their core, social movements are "essentially visual phenomena", detailed by activist clothes, posters, street performances and online viral videos (Mattoni and Teune 2014, p. 876). As such, image-making, display and circulation become a site of political contention, including, we add, the processes of capture, display and remediation within the GLAM sector. This recognition creates a central challenge for curators and caretakers of protest memory: how to build on cultural memory while situating these fleeting protest imaginaries and ephemeral productions to re-contextualise them historically; while at the same time maintaining a trained eye for messy multiplicities, conflicts and frictions. That is, to usefully expand our radical imaginaries and historical literacies of protest cultures as a form of civic and democratic engagement.

THE MEDIA-MEMORY-ACTIVISM NEXUS[3]

In approaching protest memory as a cultural technique that requires remediating the relations between humans, things and media (Siegert 2013), it is salient to consider how memory and social movement scholars have positioned the concepts of activist, protest and social movement memory. Three main trajectories are articulated within the scholarship to date: *memories of activism, memories in activism* and *memory activism*. Within these trajectories, mediation and remediation play key roles.[4] In what follows, we outline the core principles connected to these conceptualisations, while teasing out the under-articulated connections to the museum and archive sector.

Memories of Activism

Memories *of* activism refer to how protest movements are culturally remembered via representations and storytelling in media and popular culture, as well as wider commemorative activities in the public sphere. This includes via television, cinema, literature, music, fashion, theatre, advertising, visual arts and social media (Crozier-De Rosa and Mackie 2019; Reading and Katriel 2015; Robertson 2018). As social movement scholars have noted, a "central concern within this area of research is to explain how certain events are remembered and also to identify the reasons why a particular movement is remembered" (Daphi and Zamponi 2019, p. 404). As a popular mass media form, screen culture has a particular aptitude for bringing protest memories to life. There has been a boom in recent years of historical dramas depicting feminist, queer, Black power, civil rights and student organising struggles released by major studios. This demonstrates a new cultural appetite and mainstreaming of protest memories seen to have commercial appeal. Such titles include *Suffragette* (Gavron, dir. 2015a), *Misbehaviour* (Lowthorpe, dir. 2020), *Pride* (Warchus, dir. 2014), *Selma* (DuVernay, dir. 2014), *Judas and the Black Messiah* (King, dir. 2021) and *The Trial of the Chicago 7* (Sorkin, dir. 2020). These filmic representations are based on true events and archival research, but, as cultural productions, are ultimately steered by invention. Bringing protest memories (with varying degrees of historical fidelity) to new audiences and generations, screen culture has an important role in advancing schemas of social justice struggles in public imaginaries.

Placing a spotlight on how LGBTIQ+ activist histories are remembered in screen culture, Anamarija Horvat argues that "queer commemorative cinema and television can serve complex functions" (2021, p. 5). Queer screen cultures offer a source of affirmation in instances where LGBTIQ+ knowledge and acceptance may be lacking in the social frameworks of the family. Such cultural productions also help counter the lack of intergenerational knowledge and contact instigated by the AIDS crisis, in which LGBTIQ+ communities were decimated. In turn, while queer communities have worked hard to produce activist and community archives locally and nationally, "such archives are in many cases only beginning to be digitised" (2021, p. 6) and are far less accessible to the average queer person than a Hollywood film might be. To their advantage, globalised cultural productions are screened transnationally and can become available via on-demand streaming platforms—albeit with access to these mediums tempered by paywalls and films on protest and queer desire subject to censorship globally (Schoonover and Galt 2016).

With the media-memory-activism nexus in mind, we reposition the *archive as a site of cultural production*, and ultimately of protest memory. This is exemplified in the six years of archival research behind the production of the historical fiction film *Suffragette* (Gavron, dir. 2015a), a movie that rejuvenated protest memories of the British Votes for Women campaign, brought to new audiences via the A-list Hollywood stars Carey Mulligan and Meryl Streep.[5] We argue that such cultural productions exemplify how archival memory can transfer to public and popular cultural memory through remediation strategies: such texts and processes permit protest materials and stories to travel further. At the same time, the memory work and cultural labour of archivists, museum practitioners and heritage workers in making such encounters possible "has been curiously under-theorised in emerging discussions of social movement memories" to date (Chidgey 2020, p. 225). We see this in the tendency of *memories of activism* scholars to focus on cultural representations and semiotic analyses of texts, rather than on the production cultures and behind the scenes memory work that enables such cultural texts (and thus cultural memory products) to emerge. We return to archival and curatorial efforts to create memories of activism, in the case of the anti-Trump Women's March, in Chapter 4.

Memories in Activism

Memories *in* activism refer to how activists mobilise the slogans, actions, spaces, objects and memory cultures of past social movements for strategic purposes (Chidgey 2018; Griffin and McDonagh 2018; Daphi and Zamponi 2019). Mnemonic citations of past social movements are consciously invoked by activists to create strong collective identity bonds and to help place current activism within wider histories of social change. These memory acts constitute what Ron Eyerman (2016, p. 79) has termed "the performative processes of collective will formation", as movement actors generate inspiration and memory capital "by infusing themselves with history, referencing past movements and employing inherited ritual performances". This memory work bolsters feelings of belonging and intergenerational and inter-movement connections. Such memory acts also create ready-made narratives for journalists, bystanders and interested parties. This cultivation of 'usable pasts' within movements helps to confer moral legitimacy on present social struggles; this is achieved through their mnemonic proximity to struggles that have come before (and all the better if the cited struggles are high-profile, successful or well regarded). Relying on mnemonic citations to past struggles, however, can have a constraining effect, as social movement scholars have started to note (Merrill et al. 2020). Social movements must strategically 'forget' past tactics and ways of doing things, to reinvent their protest strategies and create novel forms of resistance that speak to changes in the political and media environment. This increases activist chances of keeping public and journalistic attention on them, to stir the public imagination.

Beyond semiotic and discursive appeals to past social movements by contemporary activists, we argue that *memories in activism* must also include how activists approach the memory work of documenting their movements. This is in distinction to when memory forms the central focus of activism, which is characterised as *memory activism*, as we discuss shortly. Activist relations to memory work, and the cultural labour this requires, can be highly variable. From trade unions to anti-capitalist organisations, feminist to LGBTIQ+ groups, civil rights to environmental struggles, there are a wealth of examples where activists have been key memory workers on the ground—documenting their movements, creating grassroots, community and activist archives and new information management strategies and working in collaboration with established heritage institutions to donate their records and artefacts (Cifor 2022; Cohen 2018; Lee 2016; Sheffield 2020; Withers 2015).[6] For these activists, protest memory is a vital resource that aids intergenerational knowledge, helps to build activist repertoires and skills and serves as a source of inspiration and hope. For others, tending to the documentation, preservation, exhibition and discussion of movement lives and afterlives is a distraction from the 'real work' of political activism.[7] Within activist networks, the perceived elite status of museums and archives can be deemed antithetical to the horizontal, consensus-based mode of much contemporary protest culture.[8] Even those interested in memory practices can view institutional archives and museums as 'dead' places of memory.[9] We explore this further in Chapters 4 and 5 in relation to the making of archives of activism and activist archives.

Memory Activism

Memory activism differs from the above two practices as it refers to when issues of collective remembrance, public history and commemoration are themselves the central subject and object of political activism.[10] Under these circumstances, memory practices become emblematic of cultural power and are thus highly fraught terrains of political contestation. In their state-of-the-art compendium on global memory activism, Yifat Gutman and Jenny Wüstenberg define memory activism as the *"strategic commemoration of a contested past to achieve mnemonic or political change by working outside state channels"* (2023, p. 5, emphasis in original). For these scholars, memory activism embraces the work of social movements and formal civic organisations, but also includes individuals and small groups who work in a more ad hoc fashion to achieve mnemonic change. What distinguishes *memory activism* from *memory of activism* and *memory in activism* is that memory practices and (de-)commemoration are both the means and the goal of activist practice. This is evidenced by the recent wave in which colonial-era statues and monuments to slave traders have been vandalised and toppled across Europe and the US, to enact a decolonial, anti-racist reclaiming of public memory and public space (Berger et al. 2021; Fridman 2022; Gutman and Wüstenberg 2023; Rigney 2022). It is important to maintain the distinctions between 'of' and 'in' (and also hold them together) because memory activism in any given moment is different from recognising the memories of activism and the role of memory in activism that together may have finally led to the activist moment of, for example, toppling a statue after years of frustration by activists. In addition, it should be noted that activists are often unlikely to refer to themselves as *memory activists*; this is a predominately academic term with varying grassroots currency. Moreover, activists may come to memory activism at different points in their activist biographies, including tending to their own legacies and the contested politics of collective memory with more fervour once the wider movements in which they have laboured have died down.

In the most part, memory activism has been examined through the lens of grassroots activity, with little attention paid to the potential role of cultural institutions, such as establishment museums and archives, in advancing cognisant values and methods (for an exception see Lehrer 2023; Sodaro 2023). In most discussions, memory activism is predicated upon the work of activists and civilians, but institutional actors—who may be working within or outside of state channels via heritage and memory institutions—have been sidelined. Without seeking to dilute the analytical strength of the concept of memory activism as put forward by scholars such as Gutman and Wüstenberg (2023), there is scope to bring practitioners and heritage professionals further into these discussions. We question the neat dichotomy of 'activists vs cultural and heritage practitioners', especially in this era of labour precarity and portfolio careers, in which actors may occupy multiple positions. As we have noted elsewhere and will explore in subsequent chapters: "a memory activist, scholar, curator, and practitioner may be one and the same person" (Chidgey 2023, p. 69).

Between Memory Activism, Museum Activism and Archival Activism

This leads us to consider potential synergies between memory activism and existing concepts such as *museum activism* and *archival activism*. Such interdisciplinary academic approaches are increasingly important to better understand the present "age of protest" (Raicovich 2021) which implicates the cultural and heritage sectors and their cultural workforces. Moreover, we seek to contribute a cultural sector understanding to the relative scarcity of academic attempts across disciplines to examine the 'memory-activism relationship' (Berger et al. 2021), thus bringing the important role and operations of cultural and heritage institutions further into scrutiny and critical reflection.

To begin with the emerging concept of museum activism. Museum scholars Robert Janes and Richard Sandell (2019) position museum activism within changing social expectations regarding the role and responsibility of cultural institutions. Over time, the purpose of the mainstream museum has shifted from operating as elite gatekeepers of official memory and national identity, to institutions for social inclusion, to now increasing demands to operate as institutions for equity and social and planetary justice. Janes and Sandell provide a deliberately open definition of this concept, characterising museum activism as "museum practice, shaped out of ethically informed values, that is intended to bring about political, social and environmental change" (2019, p. 1). This can refer to changing institutional practices from within—such as diversifying workforces, challenging racism, classism, sexism, homophobia and ableism in museum spaces, and re-thinking operating practices—to working with wider publics and beneficiaries in acts of co-creation and shared authority, to supporting personalised voices and visibility in social justice concerns.[11] It can also involve the museum sector speaking up against political administrations, policies and the private sector. We discuss examples of museum activism and their imbrication with memory practices further in Chapter 3.

On a macro-institutional level, a key element of museum activism is the commitment to values and institutional statements that will steer museum workers to "take action in the world" (2019, p. 9). Janes and Sandell identify the values of humility, interconnectedness, openness, empathy and resilience as central to this ethos. This creates scope for a potential alliance between museum professionals and grassroots activists. Not only in the collection, curation and memorialisation of social justice struggle, and an implicit re-distribution, or sharing, of curatorial power and museum resources with community actors, but also in the alignment of institutional voice and memory work to pressing social concerns. We argue that 'memory' (what is remembered, who is remembered, how it is remembered) can be one resource and commitment within the wider struggles of museum activism.

Generative connections can also be made to the concept of archival activism. This term has a long history of definition and debate within the archive sector. Taking the speech of the radical historian Howard Zinn at the annual meeting of the Society of American Archivists in 1970 as indicative, an ethos of archival activism is predicated on the dismantling of so-called professional neutrality; a value which also structures the museum sector.[12] As Zinn passionately expressed:

> The archivist, even more than the historian and the political scientist, tends to be scrupulous about his [sic] neutrality, and to see his job as a technical job, free from the nasty world of political interest: a job of collecting, sorting, preserving, making available, the records of the society. But I […] argue that the archivist, in subtle ways, tends to perpetuate the political and economic status quo simply by going about his ordinary business. His supposed neutrality is, in other words, a fake. If so, the rebellion of the archivist against his normal role is not, as so many scholars fear, the politicizing of a neutral craft, but the humanizing of an inevitably political craft. (Zinn 1977, p. 20)

Zinn argues that the archivist's job is to either choose to work within "the priorities and directions set by the dominant forces of society, or else to promote those human values of peace, equality, and justice, which our present society denies" (1977, p. 20). His suggested actions—to create oral histories with marginalised groups, to collect the papers of social movements, to ensure governmental transparency of archival records to aid accountability—are practices that have gained increasing traction in recent decades.[13]

Professional archivists have now developed a range of archival activist strategies. These include building community archives outside of institutional control; socially conscious work within government-funded and mainstream archives (by promoting institutional transparency and accountability); research-based activism (retracing radical or suppressed histories); and socially conscious work by institutionally independent archivists (Vukliš and Gilliland 2016). To this we add new forms of archival innovation which connects archival activism to the generation of protest memories, stories and personal accounts, and the ways in which archives are connected, remediated and part of the wider cultural conversation about protest cultures. In scope, archival activism spans both the work of professional archivists in collecting the records and material cultures of activism and making them available, and how activists themselves engage with the archivisation of their movements and activist work (see Flinn 2011; Flinn and Alexander 2015; Caswell 2021). We will examine reflections on 'archival activism' by both professional archivists and grassroots activists further in Chapters 4 and 5.

CONCLUSION

This chapter has sought to lay the groundwork for the protest memory framework that we introduce in Chapter 3, to further detail the connections between cultural labour, the GLAM sector and activist memory work. The groundwork established in this chapter has outlined the variety of ways in which protest memory occurs as a cultural technique. This spans the practices and values surrounding *memories of activism* (how remembrance of past struggles are transmitted culturally and medially, including via memory work in the archive for cultural productions), *memories in activism* (how social movements use movement memories in their protest actions and document their own movement memories) and *memory activism* (how memory practices for social transformation are constructed and fought for). We have drawn from cultural memory

studies, media and cultural studies and social movement studies to eluci-
date the relations between activism and memory and have put these
into conversation with work drawn from museum, curatorial and archive
studies on museum and archival activism. We have suggested three key
features which underpin a curatorial perspective on protest memory
collection, curation, display and interpretation: (i) the in-between state
of protest memory as both fragile and memorable; (ii) the object-image-
material connectivity of protest memory that attaches protest memorialisation to certain times, places and people (while remaining open to
new forms of re- and de-contextualisation and remediation); and (iii)
the media-memory-activism nexus that provides the cultural terrain for
protest memory to both grow or to be forgotten.

Within each of these academic considerations, cultural memory is
seen as a powerful force in which (re)mediations of the activist past are
represented in new contexts for political and social purposes. Vibrant
emotions and affects are created when remembering protest, and this
can be harnessed to further activist work (through building collective
identity, mobilising new publics, conferring moral legitimacy on public
contentions and so forth). We have suggested that producing vibrant
memory cultures has strategic benefits for protesters, their advocates and
sympathetic public and cultural institutions, offering "a vortex of recy-
cling, recollection and political action that can be summed up as 'civic
memory'" (Rigney 2018, p. 372). Such forms of civic memory strengthen
democratic engagement through the activation of 'usable pasts' of social
struggles. These memories do the cultural work of reminding audiences
of the hard-fought battles to gain rights, dignity, safety and recognition.
In this chapter we have also argued that the scope of protest memory
should be expanded; to move beyond existing accounts of grassroots
politics and the symbolic content of media productions, to include the
sphere of activity and value-creation of museum professionals, curators
and archivists who work behind the scenes. In this regard, we have argued
for a closer conversation between (inter)disciplinary work surrounding
memory activism, museum activism and archival activism. We continue
to build upon these synergies via the empirical case studies explored in
this book. More immediately, in the next chapter we explore the complex
relations between protest acts and cultural labour within the museum and
archive sector today, to advance a nuanced analytical framework of protest
memory.

NOTES

1. Ethical and legal issues involved with documenting activist online social media include: the social media platforms' shifting terms of service, the use of the archive under intellectual property laws, issues of privacy, research use and consent to collect, as well as technological changes which can cause data corruption, media and software obsolescence and inadequate metadata (Velte 2018). As Velte (2018) notes, documenting activists within existing structures may be negative for some communities, including issues of custody, colonialism and displacement for indigenous groups. Archives have been used by state agencies to conduct surveillance against protesters. Authors writing about activist curated online archives connected to the Arab Spring, for example, discuss self-censorship in archival practices to avoid putting activists at risk within violent regimes (Della Ratta et al. 2020; Chidgey 2020). Focusing on Hong Kong's Umbrella Movement Visual Archive (UMVA), Tong (2022) discusses how authoritarian governments censor political information and threaten the safety of pro-democracy citizens. This creates risks for archivists and activists alike. In sum, Velte (2018, p. 116) argues that "balancing access and privacy is a fundamental exercise for archival professionals".

2. Research demonstrates that photojournalists, as key actors within the public circulation of protest memory, routinely seek to provide images that meet expectations of media outlets on a commercial level. These include images that (i) convey the magnitude and representativeness of the protest, (ii) depict banners and other forms of material culture that demonstrate slogans and images that quickly illustrate the protest cause, (iii) capture the atmosphere of the protest, where 'good protest' is characterised by passion, collective action and energy and (iv) capture moments of violence, or threats of violence, which is the most commercially lucrative form of protest-image (Veneti 2017, p. 288). We can consider how archivists and curators seek to achieve similar aims within their collection policies and exhibitions, in terms of 'representativeness', 'illustration of cause' and 'atmosphere' (see Chapter 4).

3. Our media-memory-activism nexus is inspired by Ann Rigney's (2018) articulation of the memory-activism nexus. This nexus emphasises the connections between memory of activism, memory

in activism and memory activism. We add media to highlight the crucial role of mediation, remediation and material culture in remembering protest cultures.

4. Processes of mediation and remediation are inherent in all acts of cultural memory. "Just as there is no cultural memory prior to mediation there is no mediation without remediation: all representations of the past draw on available media technologies, on existent media products, on patterns of representation and medial aesthetics" (Erll and Rigney 2012, p. 4).

5. See Gavron (2015b) for an account of the six years of research behind the production of the British historical fiction film *Suffragette* (Gavron, dir. 2015a). This research spanned consultations with historians, archivists, curators and archival research based at the National Archives, Museum of London, the Women's Library, British Library, British Film Institute, British Pathé, Getty and Gaunt International Archives. While a vivid example of *memory of activism*, promotion for the film generated a backlash around racial politics after white cast members appeared in T-shirts emblazoned with the slogan "I'd rather be a rebel than a slave", a quote from a 1913 speech by Votes for Women leader Emmeline Pankhurst (1858–1928).

6. Activists have long explored autobiography as a site of activist memory work, see Perkins (2000). Oral history, too, has a central role to play in creating memory work within and about social movements. This method traditionally foregrounds the lived experience of marginalised and ordinary citizens, to enact a 'history from below', as a rejoinder to the exclusions of the historical record that favours a history of the elites (Shopes and Hamilton 2008). When it comes to activism, oral history has been used as a historical memory technique to document experiences from participants in social movement struggles, whose involvements are often occluded from news media and other forms of public history documentation. Oral history projects have been deployed within feminist social struggles, for example, ensuring that women's voices and political mobilisations are recognised and accounted for in the historic record, including their many contestations around race, class, sexuality and dis/ability and the multitude of social differences within political movements. As the oral historian Margaretta Jolly recounts, oral histories offer "a fuller social and emotional

history" of protest and resistance, "helping to structure a realistic as well as hopeful version of this complex collective past" (2019, pp. 6, 9).

7. The lack of importance to memory work was evident in the struggles of archivist-activists in the Occupy Wall Street (OWS) movement. As Kylie Message documented via her ethnography of OWS archiving initiatives, the General Assembly rejected applications from the OWS archival working group for resources such as storage boxes and storage space. Here the "movement's lack of interest in using traditional institutions and forms of media to co-opt or subvert mainstream news outlets or sites of representation (including museums, archives, and libraries) over the long term contrasted with their priority for having a current impact" (2020, p. 97).

8. As Joan Nestle wrote in 1979, outlining the central values of the activist-led, autonomous Lesbian Herstory Archives in New York (1974–present): "The archives should be housed within the community, not an academic campus that is by definition closed to many women. The archives should share the political and cultural world of its people and not be located in an isolated building that continues to exist while its community dies...The archives should be involved in the political struggles of the Lesbian people, a place where ideas and experiences from the past interact with the living issues of the Lesbian community...The archives should be staffed by Lesbians so the collection will always have a living cultural context. Archival skills shall be taught, one generation of Lesbians to another, breaking [the] elitism of traditional archives...Its atmosphere must be nourishing, entry into our archives should be entry into a caring home" (1979, p. 11).

9. As Stefan Dickers, Special Collections and Archives Manager at Bishopsgate Institute, London, told us during an expert panel: "If activists know their archive is going to be accessible and used, engaged and celebrated, they're a lot more keen to give papers, rather than to somewhere it's going to be in a box and out the way" (Dickers 2019).

10. Fruitful comparisons can be made between this emergent concept of memory activism and more established examinations of activist dedications to public history and 'history from below', especially since the late 1960s and 1970s, as a way to counter the elitism

and exclusions of the historic record (see Kelland 2018; Meringolo 2021).

11. The mainstreaming of activism in the arts and cultural sector has been met with cynicism. *ArtNet* declared 'activism' as one of the art world's most overused words (Judah 2016). Curators Catherine Flood and Gavin Grindon (2014, p. 10) similarly caution that 'activism' has functioned "as an enclosure of cultural value, authenticity, and impact on the part of professional artists, critics, designers, corporations and even NGOs". This details how cultural institutions who claim activism in the work that they do, or who showcase professional artists, can risk overlooking grassroots creatives and activist social movements; key constituencies whose presence and work are harder to 'capture' and represent in ethical and authentic ways in the cultural and heritage sector.

12. Arguments for the inherent non-neutrality of archival work find their counterpart in the international museum sector. See the advocacy campaign #MuseumsAreNotNeutral, spearheaded in 2017 by the museum practitioners La Tanya S. Autry and Mike Murawski.

13. As part of the centennial celebration of Howard Zinn's birth, archivists, educators and historians congregated online for a roundtable event on Radicalizing the Archives, prompted by Zinn's 1970 speech at the Society of American Archivists. For a record of these proceedings, see https://www.zinnedproject.org/news/radicalizing-the-archives.

References

Berger, S., S. Scalmer, and C. Wicke, eds. 2021. *Remembering Social Movements: Activism and Memory*. Abingdon: Routledge.

Castells, M. 2015. *Networks of Outrage and Hope: Social Movements in the Internet Age*, 2nd ed. Cambridge: Polity Press.

Caswell, M. 2021. *Urgent Archives: Enacting Liberatory Memory Work*. New York: Routledge.

Chidgey, R. 2018. *Feminist Afterlives: Assemblage Memory in Activist Times*. Cham: Palgrave Macmillan.

Chidgey, R. 2020. How to Curate a 'Living Archive': The Restlessness of Activist Time and Labour. In *Social Movements, Cultural Memory and Digital Media:*

Mobilising Mediated Remembrance, ed. S. Merrill, E. Keightley, and P. Daphi, 225–248. Cham: Palgrave Macmillan.

Chidgey, R. 2023. Intersectionality and Memory Activism. In *The Routledge Companion of Memory Activism*, ed. Y. Gutman and J. Wüstenberg, 65–69. New York: Routledge.

Cifor, M. 2022. *Viral Cultures: Activist Archiving in the Age of AIDS*. Minneapolis: University of Minnesota Press.

Cohen, P. 2018. *Archive That, Comrade! Left Legacies and the Counter Culture of Remembrance*. Oakland: PM Press.

Coody Cooper, K. 2008. *Spirited Encounters: American Indians Protest Museum Policies and Practices*. Lanham: AltaMira Press.

Crozier-De Rosa, S., and V. Mackie, eds. 2019. *Remembering Women's Activism*. Abingdon: Routledge.

Cvetkovich, A. 2003. *An Archive of Feelings: Trauma, Sexuality, and Lesbian Public Cultures*. Durham: Duke University Press.

Daphi, P., and L. Zamponi. 2019. Exploring the Movement-Memory Nexus: Insights and Ways Forward. *Mobilization: An International Quarterly* 24 (4): 399–417.

Della Ratta, D., K. Dickinson, and S. Haugbolle, eds. 2020. *The Arab Archives: Mediated Memories and Digital Flows*. Amsterdam: Institute of Network Cultures.

Dickers, S. 2019. Roundtable Talk: Future Directions—Activist Museums Panel. *Curating Protest Memory Expert Workshop*, March 28. King's College London.

Duncombe, S., ed. 2002. *Cultural Resistance Reader*. London: Verso.

DuVernay, A. dir. 2014. *Selma*.

Edy, J. 1999. Journalistic Use of Collective Memory. *Journal of Communication* 49 (2): 71–85.

Erll, A., and A. Rigney. 2012. Introduction: Cultural Memory and its Dynamics. In *Mediation, Remediation, and the Dynamics of Cultural Memory*, ed. A. Erll and A. Rigney, 1–11. Berlin: De Gruyter.

Eyerman, R. 2016. Social Movements and Memory. In *Routledge International Handbook of Memory Studies*, ed. A.L. Tota and T. Hagen, 79–83. Abingdon: Routledge.

Feigenbaum, A. 2014. Resistant Matters: Tents, Tear Gas and the "Other Media" of Occupy. *Communication and Critical/Cultural Studies* 11 (1): 15–24.

Flinn, A. 2011. Archival Activism: Independent and Community-Led Archives, Radical Public History and the Heritage Professions. *InterActions: UCLA Journal of Education and Information Studies* 7: 2. Available: https://doi.org/10.5070/D472000699. Accessed 9 Oct 2022.

Flinn, A., and B. Alexander. 2015. "Humanizing an Inevitability Political Craft": Introduction to the Special Issue on Archiving Activism and Activist Archiving. *Archival Science* 15 (4): 329–335.

Flood, C., and G. Grindon. 2014. Introduction. In *Disobedient Objects*, ed. C. Flood and G. Grindon, 6–25. London: V&A Publishing.

Fridman, O. 2022. *Memory Activism and Digital Practices after Conflict: Unwanted Memories*. Amsterdam: Amsterdam University Press.

Gavron, S. dir. 2015a. *Suffragette*.

Gavron, S. 2015b. The Making of the Feature Film Suffragette. *Women's History Review* 24 (6): 985–995.

Giannini, T. 2019. Contested Space: Activism and Protest. In *Museums and Digital Culture*, ed. T. Giannini and J.P. Bowen, 91–111. Cham: Springer.

Griffin, C., and B. McDonagh, eds. 2018. *Remembering Protest in Britain Since 1500: Memory, Materiality and the Landscape*. Cham: Palgrave Macmillan.

Gutiérrez, M. 2018. *Data Activism and Social Change*. Cham: Palgrave Macmillan.

Gutman, Y., and J. Wüstenberg, eds. 2023. *The Routledge Companion of Memory Activism*. New York: Routledge.

Hajek, A., C. Lohmeier, and C. Pentzold, eds. 2016. *Memory in a Mediated World: Remembrance and Reconstruction*. Basingstoke: Palgrave Macmillan.

Harrebye, S. 2016. *Social Change and Creative Activism in the 21st Century*. Basingstoke: Palgrave Macmillan.

Hirsch, M. 2019. Introduction: Practicing Feminism, Practicing Memory. In *Women Mobilizing Memory*, ed. A.G. Altınay, M.J. Contreras, M. Hirsch, J. Howard, B. Karaca, and A. Solomon, 1–23. New York: Columbia University Press.

Horvat, A. 2021. *Screening Queer Memory: LGBTQ Pasts in Contemporary Film and Television*. London: Bloomsbury.

Janes, R.R., and R. Sandell, eds. 2019. *Museum Activism*. London: Routledge.

Jasper, J. 1997. *The Art of Moral Protest: Culture, Biography, and Creativity in Social Movements*. Chicago: University of Chicago Press.

Jolly, M. 2019. *Sisterhood and After: An Oral History of the UK Women's Liberation Movement, 1968–Present*. Oxford: Oxford University Press.

Joyce, M. 2010. *Digital Activism Decoded: The New Mechanism of Change*. New York: International Debate Education Association.

Judah, H. 2016. The 13 Most Overused Words in the Art World in 2016. *Artnet*, December 28. Available: https://news.artnet.com/art-world/13-words-the-art-world-overused-792455. Accessed 9 Oct 2022.

Kelland, L.L. 2018. *Clio's Foot Soldiers: Twentieth-Century US Social Movements and Collective Memory*. Amherst: University of Massachusetts Press.

King, S. dir. 2021. *Judas and the Black Messiah*.

Lee, D. 2016. *Activist Archives: Youth Culture and the Political Past in Indonesia*. Durham: Duke University Press.

Lehrer, E. 2023. Museums and 'Curatorial Activism.' In *The Routledge Companion of Memory Activism*, ed. Y. Gutman and J. Wüstenberg, 373–380. New York: Routledge.

Lekakis, E. 2022. *Consumer Activism: Promotional Culture and Resistance*. London: Sage.

Lowthorpe, P. dir. 2020. *Misbehaviour*.

Mattoni, A., and S. Teune. 2014. Visions of Protest: A Media-Historic Perspective on Images in Social Movements. *Sociology Compass* 8 (6): 876–887.

Meikle, G. 2018. Introduction: Making Meanings and Making Trouble. In *The Routledge Companion to Media and Activism*, ed. G. Meikle, 1–16. New York: Routledge.

Meringolo, D., ed. 2021. *Radical Roots: Public History and a Tradition of Social Justice Activism*. Amherst: Amherst College Press. Available: https://www.ful crum.org/concern/monographs/rf55z988p [accessed 9 October 2022]

Merrill, S., E. Keightley, and P. Daphi, eds. 2020. *Social Movements, Cultural Memory and Digital Media: Mobilising Mediated Remembrance*. Basingstoke: Palgrave Macmillan.

Message, K. 2020. *Collecting Activism, Archiving Occupy Wall Street*. New York: Routledge.

Murawski, M. 2021. *Museums as Agents of Change: A Guide to Becoming a Changemaker*. Lanham: Rowman & Littlefield.

Nestle, J. 1979. Notes on Radical Archiving from a Lesbian Feminist Standpoint. *Gay Insurgent* 4–5: 11.

Perkins, M.V. 2000. *Autobiography as Activism: Three Black Women of the Sixties*. Jackson: University of Mississippi Press.

Raicovich, L. 2021. *Culture Strike: Art and Museum in an Age of Protest*. London: Verso.

Reading, A., and T. Katriel, eds. 2015. *Cultural Memories of Nonviolent Struggles: Powerful Times*. Basingstoke: Palgrave Macmillan.

Rigney, A. 2018. Remembering Hope: Transnational Activism Beyond the Traumatic. *Memory Studies* 11 (3): 368–380.

Rigney, A. 2020. Mediations of Outrage: How Violence Against Protestors is Remembered. *Social Research: An International Quarterly* 87 (3): 707–733.

Rigney, A. 2022. Toxic Monuments and Mnemonic Regime Change. *Studies on National Movements* 9: 1. Available: https://openjournals.ugent.be/snm/art icle/id/85270. Accessed 9 Oct 2022.

Rigney, A., and T. Smits, eds. 2023. *The Visual Memory of Protest*. Amsterdam: Amsterdam University Press.

Robertson, A., ed. 2018. *Screening Protest: Visual Narratives of Dissent Across Time, Space and Genre*. London: Routledge.

Robertson, K. 2019. *Tear Gas Epiphanies. Protest, Culture, Museums*. Montreal: McGill-Queen's University Press.

Schoonover, K., and R. Galt. 2016. *Queer Cinema in the World*. Durham: Duke University Press.

Serafini, P., J. Holtaway, and A. Cossu, eds. 2018. *ArtWORK. Art, Labour and Activism*. London: Rowman & Littlefield.

Sheffield, R.T. 2020. *Documenting Rebellions: A Study of Four Lesbian and Gay Archives*. Sacramento: Litwin Books.

Shopes, L., and P. Hamilton, eds. 2008. *Oral History and Public Memories*. Philadelphia: Temple University Press.

Siegert, B. 2013. Cultural Techniques: Or the End of the Intellectual Postwar Era in German Media Theory. *Theory, Culture & Society* 30 (6): 48–65.

Sodaro, A. 2023. Museums. In *The Routledge Companion of Memory Activism*, ed. Y. Gutman and J. Wüstenberg, 213–217. New York: Routledge.

Sorkin, A. dir. 2020. *The Trial of the Chicago 7*.

Tong, K.-L. 2022. Archiving Social Movement Memories Amidst Autocratization: A Case Study of Hong Kong's Umbrella Movement Visual Archive. *International Journal of Heritage Studies* 28 (6): 733–751.

Velte, Ashlyn. 2018. Ethical Challenges and Current Practices in Activist Social Media Archives. *The American Archivist* 81 (1): 112–134.

Veneti, A. 2017. Aesthetics of Protest: An Examination of the Photojournalistic Approach to Protest Imagery. *Visual Communication* 16 (3): 279–298.

Vukliš, V., and A.J. Gilliland. 2016. Archival Activism: Emerging Forms, Local Applications. In *Archives in the Service of People—People in the Service of Archives*, ed. B. Filej, 14–25. Maribor: Alma Mater Europea.

Warchus, M., dir. 2014. *Pride*.

White, M. 2016. *The End of Protest: A New Playbook for Revolution*. Toronto: Knopf Canada.

Withers, D.M. 2015. *Feminism, Digital Culture and the Politics of Transmission: Theory, Practice and Cultural Heritage*. London: Rowman & Littlefield.

Zinn, H. 1977. Secrecy, Archives and the Public Interest. *The Midwestern Archivist* 2 (2): 14–26.

CHAPTER 3

Towards a Protest Memory Framework

Abstract This chapter offers a new analytical framework for understanding the creation and securitisation of protest memory, grounded within practitioner-based examples and projects. Drawing on examples from within the UK and internationally, we discuss five axes of protest memory as they are produced within the cultural sector. We identify museums and archives as (i) sites of protest, (ii) agents of protest, (iii) domains of protest memory, (iv) co-creators of protest memory and (v) protectors, carers and innovators of protest memory. Via this analytical framework, we position protest memory, and the will to act on social issues, as an ethos that implicates institutional frameworks. Ultimately, we argue that an institutional *protest memory ethos* assembles cultural and heritage professionals, artists, activists, academics, citizens, technologies, material objects and immaterial assets in complex memory work in the service of wider social justice claims.

Keywords Memory institutions · Heritage professionals · Cultural sector · Care · Civic memory

R. Chidgey and J. Garde-Hansen, *Museums, Archives and Protest Memory*, Palgrave Macmillan Memory Studies, https://doi.org/10.1007/978-3-031-44478-4_3

INTRODUCTION

Further attention is required to understand the complexity of protest memory curation and circulation in the arts, heritage and cultural sectors, and the role of museums and archives as agents and intermediaries in this work. While curatorial and cultural studies have attended to art activism and the exhibition of protest (see, among others, Reed 2019; Williams 2017), and archive studies to the collection, preservation, display and engagement with protest artefacts for the historical record (Cooper 1987; Hoyer and Almeida 2021; Flinn 2011), there is scant work that examines the role of cultural institutions as potential *protest memory agents*. That is, the active roles that museums and archives can adopt in not only collecting and caring for protest artefacts and records, but in actively promoting protest sensibilities from within and beyond their walls. This leads us to examine how cultural institutions, in practice, can enact and facilitate interweaving, complex and contentious forms of museum, archive and institutional memory activisms.

This necessitates a rethinking of memory's traditional place within the museum and archive sector. Such a revisioning moves us beyond a common-sense understanding of the museum or archive as a "cultural memory bank" (Janes and Sandell 2019, p. 11). Instead, it leads us to consider these organisations in more dynamic and generative ways. In what follows, we explore the implications for creating and curating protest memories within museum and archive spaces more widely. As part of our contribution towards a protest memory framework that thinks in close connection with the cultural sector, we identify museums and archives as (i) sites of protest, (ii) agents of protest, (iii) domains of protest memory, (iv) co-creators of protest memory and (v) protectors, carers and innovators of protest memory. In what follows we outline these five axes in more detail and provide further empirical examples within Table 3.1.

We argue that approaching museums and archives as *sites of protest* focuses attention on what kinds of activist-driven protest acts are happening at these cultural locations. Attending to museums and archives as *agents of protest*, sensitises us to how cultural institutions are enacting agential and advocacy positions, actively speaking out on social justice issues and against political administrations. Locating museums and archives as *domains of protest memory*, enables us to see how protest memory collection, curation and interpretation happen within institutions, often in ways in which authoritative power is still structurally

Table 3.1 Classifying protest acts and acts of protest memory at museums and archives

Museums and archives as…	Dynamics	Techniques	Examples
Sites of protest	Protest through the cultural institution Protest against the cultural institution	▲ Attacks on artworks; Peaceful occupation and assembly at the site ▲ Boycotting museums and art galleries and their collections and sponsors; Activist performances at the site	• Artist Tony Shafrazi uses spray paint to vandalise Picasso's *Guernica* (1937) in the Museum of Modern Art (1974), to protest how US army officials avoided prosecution for civilian massacres during the Vietnam War • Liberate Tate—collective creative disobedience ends BP sponsorship of the arts (2010–2016, UK) • *Just Stop Oil*—climate protesters throw foodstuff at artworks and superglue themselves to frames, in protest for UK disinvestment in fossil fuel (2022) • Nan Goldin forms P.A.I.N (Prescription Addiction Intervention Now) in 2017 with other artists. They target New York's Metropolitan Museum of Art (2018) and Guggenheim (2019) to protest philanthropic links to the Sackler family and their role in the US opioid crisis

(continued)

Table 3.1 (continued)

Museums and archives as...	Dynamics	Techniques	Examples
Agents of protest	Cultural institutions protest policies, administrations and world events. Encouraging audiences to campaign and protest injustice	▲ Re-hanging exhibitions in connection to current protest campaigns or current events ▲ Campaigns that draw together civil society, universities, activists and social media to address 'big problems', i.e. gentrification, capitalism, poverty, state violence	• The Museum of Modern Art, New York, rehangs its Modern galleries (2017), swapping out work by canonical Western artists for works by artists from the Muslim-majority countries affected by President Trump's travel ban • Staff, residents and allies protest against the eviction threat to the Museu da Maré, the first favela museum in Brazil, established in 2006, and threatened with closure to make way for the 2016 Olympics in Rio de Janeiro • The People's History Museum (Manchester) commits to a #AntiRefugeeLaw pledge, following a local consultation. The PHM works with campaigning and advocacy groups and those with lived experience to take a vocal stand against UK anti-refugee laws

Museums and archives as...	Dynamics	Techniques	Examples
Domains of protest memory	Collections Exhibitions Programming Learning activities	▲ Received donations of activist materials and papers; digitising activist collections ▲ Curating activism and social justice exhibitions from institutional collections ▲ Talks, workshops, events and tours pertaining to protest, activism, social justice and social movement collections, artefacts and exhibits ▲ Teacher packs, tours and institutional visits, linking collections and exhibits to national curriculums and educational programmes	• Online exhibition *When I Remember I See Red: American Indian Art and Activism in California*, Autry Museum of the American West (2022) • Digitised and searchable documents pertaining to abortion rights activism, Museum of Contraception and Abortion, Vienna, Austria (https://muvs.org) • The Center for the Study of Political Graphics archive holds 90,000 human rights and protest posters and prints (https://www.politicalgraphics.org) • The Victoria and Albert Museum (London) collection of Extinction Rebellion woodblocks and prints is interpreted by curator Corinna Gardner for schools and colleges through a YouTube video (2021)

(continued)

Table 3.1 (continued)

Museums and archives as...	Dynamics	Techniques	Examples
Co-creators of protest memory	Contemporary collecting strategies Community participation and co-creation Outreach	▲ Rapid response collecting ▲ Co-production and co-creation of protest memory in archival description, visual and digital archive development, oral history production, exhibitions and remixed archival film footage with activists and communities	• Placards, photographs and accounts from activists who marched in Black Lives Matter demonstrations in Wales on display at St Fagans National Museum of History, Amgueddfa Cymru (2020) • The Living Museums project, delivered by Children in Scotland (2021), uses curating as a method to make museums more reflective of young people's views. For the exhibition *Generation Change: Young People's Participation in Protest*, young people co-create an exhibition and publication based on young people's engagement with anti-racist, environmental and feminist protest across the UK • The Archiwum Protestów Publicznych (Archive of Public Protests) is an open-access digital archive of protest photographs in Poland post 2015, set up by photographers to create a non-commercial platform for users to reuse protest imagery (https://archiwumprotestow.pl)

Museums and archives as...	Dynamics	Techniques	Examples
Protectors, carers and innovators of protest memory	Harnessing synergies between digital, creative and museum communities Developing contemporary preservation and exhibition policies and practices Decolonising, de-carbonising and queering museums and archives	▲ Artist commissions to creatively respond to (activist) collections and materials ▲ Digital innovation in exhibition display, archival creation, meta-data, finding aids and interpretation, including the use of virtual reality, augmented reality, AI ▲ Training communities, activists and volunteers to produce, archive, conserve, exhibit and interpret protest materials ▲ Institutions holding activist materials until needed for protests	• In 2022 Tate Britain commissioned artist Keith Piper to address the protests surrounding the racist 1927 mural *The Expedition in Pursuit of Rare Meats* that covers the restaurant wall • The Australian Museum develops an immersive 360-degree virtual reality tour of *Unsettled* (2021), an indigenous-led exhibition, showcasing First Nations political movements. The immersive experience generates new forms of embodied and virtual engagement with protest memories, with VR mediation being highly memorable for the visitor (https://australian.museum/learn/first-nations/unsettled) • The University of North Carolina launches its *Archivist in a* Backpack project (2018, US), providing community partners with essential equipment and knowledge for oral history and archive production • Bishopsgate Institute (London) allows donors to check out accessioned archival materials for protest actions and then return items to the archive

located in institutional expertise. When museums and archives operate as *co-creators of protest memory*, they take a more collaborative or pro-active stance—including through methodologies such as rapid response collecting or pursuing acts of co-production with wider communities and activist knowledge holders. Finally, when cultural institutions (or individual cultural workers) act as *protectors, carers and innovators of protest memory*, they marshal their resources, including digital media capabilities, to help transform museum and archive practices.

It is important to note that the work of museums and archives can slip in-between the different classifications we propose here and can occupy different axes simultaneously and partially. Moreover, the social function of museums and archives—as agents of change, as agents of public trust and as agents of (non)neutrality—continues to be debated within the public sphere. While we have attempted such a mapping, we are by no means illustrating this in a completist manner, nor are we able to cover every technique and dynamic in the case study chapters that follow. Our framework aims to be a starting point for researchers and cultural actors to locate protest memory as a subject of study and an object for professional attention in the arts, heritage and cultural sector. The aim of this framework is to further understand what key factors and conditions are implicated when cultural institutions elect to undertake a *protest memory ethos*, aligning their values, mission statements, operating practices and activities to a cultural commons of social justice work.

Museums and Archives as Sites of Protest (See Table 3.1, Row 1)

We begin our framework by recognising that museums and galleries, with their "singular combination of historical consciousness, sense of place, and public accessibility" (Janes and Sandell 2019, p. 17), have long been targeted by activists and protesters as *sites of protest* (axis 1). Such acts of contention have unfolded through two, sometimes interweaving modalities: *protest through the museum* and *protest against the museum*. Within the first modality, protest through the museum refers to the ways in which social movement actors, artists and citizens have used museums as symbolic locations to carry out contentious politics, to air grievances and to make demands on wider social issues. We can turn to the British Votes for Women campaign of the early twentieth century to see this strategy in action. This modality is infamously captured in the action of the militant suffragette Mary Richardson, who in 1914 attacked Diego Velázquez's *Rokeby Venus* (1647–1651) in the London National Gallery with a concealed meat cleaver. Richardson's intent was to draw attention to the suffrage cause and the ill-treatment of its political prisoners. Over a century later, we see similar tactics at work within the current spate of actions in galleries and museums by the climate activists Just Stop Oil, who have thrown food stuff and protested at iconic artworks (including replicating Richardson's action with emergency rescue hammers) to escalate action on fossil fuels and the climate emergency.

With different aims and means at their disposal, these two movements have consciously selected art museums as sites of protest due to their institutional status as "repositories of high profile, financially valuable material objects" (MacLeod 2007, p. 53). This symbolic (and economic) status guarantees maximum media attention to the activist cause and leverages moral arguments about value (what is worth more, a painting or human life?). While the suffragettes staged their protests *through* the museum, the Just Stop Oil activists also directed their attention *against* the museum. This activist organisation has called on the cultural sector to "address the urgency of action. It is immoral for cultural institutions to stand by and watch whilst our society faces inevitable collapse. We call on everyone involved in arts, heritage and culture to join us in civil resistance" (Just Stop Oil 2023). We must pair this demand with wider calls within academia and museum practice, to demonstrate public advocacy and what in Chapter 6 we call 'holistic accountability'. This is to "take a stand on issues where the museum can add perspective, expertise, advice and assistance" and, we add, to insist not only on "the accountability of government and the private sector" (Janes and Sandell 2019, p. 15), but also accountability within the cultural sector.

This leads us to the second modality within the axis of museums and archives as sites of protest: *protest against the museum*. Within this modality, activists (and cultural workers who become activists) target cultural institutions for their internal policies and actions. The aim is to improve museum working practices, administration and governance. As museum scholar and practitioner Laura Raicovich notes, "protestors and unionizers are the greatest collaborators to remake museums right now" (2021, p. 167). Our observation that protests in and against museums have gained in intensity in recent years was a central motivation for writing this book. It prompted our desire to link these actions to wider concerns of cultural memory, activism and civic engagement. As we have indicated in earlier chapters, substantive protest issues within the cultural sector span ethical issues of sponsorship (e.g., oil sponsorship of the arts, the Sackler endowments); museum governance, the privileged and narrow make-up of museum staff and trustees, issues of living wages for museum staff and the employment precarity of cultural workers (see the GULF Labour—Gulf Ultra Luxury Faction occupations); and the epistemic violence foundational to many collections and subsequent calls for repatriation and reparations (highlighted by the Decolonize This Place movement).[1]

Activism against the museum has become increasingly sophisticated and artful in the new millennium. This is illustrated well in the guerrilla art performances of Liberate Tate (2010–2016) who agitated to disinvest UK art institutions from oil sponsorship. In a 2012 action entitled *The Gift*, over 100 members of Liberate Tate delivered a 16.5 metre, one and a half tonne wind turbine blade to the Tate Modern's Turbine Hall. The collective declared the turbine blade an artwork in the tradition of ready-made art. In strategy, these activists cleverly drew on the provisions of the UK government's Museums and Galleries Act of 1992, which stipulated that any 'gift to the nation' must be formally considered as part of a museum's permanent collection. While the Tate Board of Trustees ultimately declined the strategic donation, they gained permission from Liberate Tate to house photographs and documentation of *The Gift* performance in the Tate Archive.[2] This institutional response has wider implications for protest memory. As Kirsty Robertson notes in her erudite analysis of protest actions through and against Canadian museums across the twentieth century, while most museums "collect newspaper clippings pertaining to their exhibitions, most do not collect ephemera from protests that take place against them" (2019, p. 26). We concur that major museums should collect material from protests taking place at their institutions. This memory work not only demonstrates institutional reflexivity but generates a complex, potent archive of protest memory in connection with the cultural sector, which would otherwise run the risk of being lost to the public record once media headlines had died down.

MUSEUMS AND ARCHIVES AS AGENTS
OF PROTEST (SEE TABLE 3.1, ROW 2)

Moving beyond being the targets of protest actions, this axis refers to how cultural institutions are increasingly becoming *agents of protest* (axis 2). In recent years, many museums have expanded their role in culture and society to actively speak up about governmental and world problems, taking a visible stand against political administrations. These actions take the shape of coordinated demonstrations against discriminatory policies and government protocols. Protests have emerged around issues such as cuts to cultural funding which threaten the livelihood of the museum and archive sector, and actions which attempt to draw attention to the cultural value and necessity of art, culture and heritage, within political climates in which these values are undermined.

A high-profile example of coordinated action occurred in response to President Donald Trump's 2017 executive order, which banned people from six Muslim-majority countries from entering the US. Over 100 museums filed documents in court, arguing that the policy threatened their mission "to serve the public by making great works of art, representing the full range of human experiences", as Trump's executive order prevented individuals crucial to the production of exhibitions, performances and other museum events from entering the country (Stapley-Brown 2017). Later, during the height of the Covid-19 pandemic, more than 70 museums and cultural institutions in the Netherlands defied government lock-down orders and reopened their galleries as pop-up nail salons, barber shops and gyms. This one-day protest was coordinated in response to the Dutch government's inconsistent Covid-19 restrictions, whereby cultural institutions remained closed while beauty salons and gyms were permitted to open. In a playful act of civil disobedience, patrons could choose from several Van Gogh-inspired nail designs at the Van Gogh Museum in Amsterdam, barbers offered haircuts during orchestra rehearsals at the Amsterdam Royal Concert Hall, and visitors could engage in yoga sessions among paintings at the Amsterdam Museum (McGreevy 2022).

Radical action by an individual museum occurred in 2012 when the director of the Casoria Contemporary Art Museum in Naples, Italy, began burning works of art (with the consent of artists) as a provocation against cuts to arts funding and the financial precarity of public art museums (Hopper 2012). One of the artists (Severine Bourguignon) watched in support on Skype as their artwork was set on fire, thus making use of the affordances of digital and social media that museums, galleries and archives increasingly employ to perform their roles as agents of protest. Indeed, during the Black Lives Matter (BLM) protests in 2020, the Museum of London (MoL) engaged Twitter users on the protest actions circulating around the statue of Robert Milligan, a slave trader, erected on their grounds. As the MoL tweeted, the statue had "stood uncomfortably outside the Museum of London Docklands for a long time" (Fig. 3.1).[3] Seeking to also highlight the Museum of London Docklands' (MoLD) exhibition on the history of the transatlantic slave trade (and the sugar warehouse buildings of the museum) through a thread of tweets, the MoL simultaneously operated as a *site of protest* for racial justice protesters denouncing the statue's celebration of colonial histories and violence in the public sphere (axis 1), an *agent of protest* as the museum agitated for the statue's removal on the grounds of its historic links to colonial violence and exploitation (axis 2), and a *domain of protest memory* (axis 3) as the MoL remediated BLM protest actions to wider audiences through social media. The museum will likely remediate anti-racist and anti-colonial protest memories further as a *co-creator of protest memory* (axis 4) as, since March 2022, the removed statue has become part of the MoLD's permanent collection for re-contextualisation following a public consultation.[4]

MUSEUMS AND ARCHIVES AS DOMAINS OF PROTEST MEMORY (SEE TABLE 3.1, ROW 3)

Museums and archives operate as *domains of protest memory* (axis 3) where past and present social movements, protest events and activist cultures are presented and contextualised to audiences through institutional collections, curation, public programmes, learning activities, exhibitions and remediation strategies on digital and social media platforms. Typically, protest artefacts and collections come into the cultural institution's domain through donations from the private collections of activist individuals and groups. As discussed in Chapter 2, there can be nuanced factors influencing how receptive activists are to donating their materials and records (and how open the institution is to accepting the acquisition), including the nature of their cause, the perceived success of the movement, the 'fit' with the institution, whether the movement is dormant, disbanded or still active, and the significance given to memorialisation

Museum of London ✔ @MuseumofLondon · 9 Jun 2020   ···
The statue of Robert Milligan has stood uncomfortably outside the Museum
of London Docklands for a long time, one of only three museums in the UK
to address the history of the transatlantic slave trade. (thread)

![Statue of Robert Milligan covered with a cloth and a "BLACK LIVES MATTER" sign, outside the Museum of London Docklands]

    ılıl   ○ 86   ↱ 787   ♡ 1,580   ⇧

Fig. 3.1 Tweet from Museum of London, posted 9 June 2020

by activists as part of their protest repertoires. As our case study on the
environmental protest movement Platform will show (Chapter 5), the 'fit'
between protest movement and museum or archive is not always snug.

In elaborating museums and archives as a *domain of protest memory*,
we emphasise the ways in which the expertise of practitioners and institutions remain central and structural in engagements with protest cultures.

We invoke the place-based metaphor of 'domain', as the physical building of the cultural institution and its online presence, alongside its established operating practices, to foreground approaches in which protest memory collection, description, display and engagement operate in similar ways as to other collections—albeit with the recognition that protest materials, due to their unstable materiality, may present unique preservation challenges. This axis positions heritage workers as the key agents and authors of collection, display and interpretation, typically working without extensive consultation or collaboration with knowledge holders and activist communities. We see evidence of this axis in the manifold archives and museums internationally that hold protest collections, and in the surge of exhibitions surrounding protest design and artefacts in national and local museums in recent years.

We further invoke this axis to refer to display techniques that remain tonally within the professional practices of established museum institutions, and in which the intangible aspects of protest cultures (the affective, subversive states) remain muted. We share this critique to aid heritage, cultural and memory workers to better understand what makes a successful exhibition of protest. Take, for example, the reception of the British Museum's exhibition dedicated to world history and dissent, *I Object* (2018–2019), sponsored by Citibank. This exhibition started with a compelling premise: the *Private Eye* editor Ian Hislop was invited to hand-pick a range of objects from the British Museum's collection which spoke to the idea of subversion and satire. Over 100 objects were selected. They ranged from crafted oak doors from Nigeria, made to celebrate the 1924 British Empire Exhibition, and which featured satirical carved images of British colonialists, to a £20 note defaced with the rubber-stamped slogan "STAY IN THE EU", which protested the 2016 UK 'Brexit' referendum. *I Object* attempted innovation with its display strategies. The institution's curatorial wall text was supplemented by speech bubbles from Hislop, underscoring his reaction to the object selected. However, as noted in art reviews, the exhibition was declared "joyless in the extreme", through what art critics called "the strait-laced presentation of objects in cases" (Jones 2018). The exhibition was deemed to create "the opposite of a subversive mood" (ibid.). The homogenisation of dissent globally in the *I Object* exhibition, without nuanced context, was also perceived by reviewers as ahistorical, didactic and mnemonically flat. We note the difficulties of capturing the spirit of dissent and protest movements, their joy and subversion, as well as their intangible affective states and social networks, as central difficulties for curators of protest memory. This includes exhibition strategies capable of conveying the ludic—or spontaneously playful—dimension of protest objects and artefacts (Rees 2019).

Finally, in approaching museums and archives as domains of protest memory, further thought can be given to the benefits of a more passive collection policy. This is in distinction to participatory contemporary collecting and rapid response initiatives that we will later discuss. It is useful to clarify terms here. Contemporary collecting refers to collecting initiatives (of objects, stories and material culture) that respond to events of the recent past or those within 'living memory' of up to fifty years (Kavanagh 2019). These projects can be undertaken in partnership with communities with lived experience. They offer the opportunity for institutions to address gaps within their existing collections and to spotlight and amplify the voices of historically marginalised social groups—an important agenda item within museum and archival activism. Active versus passive collecting are two central methodologies driving contemporary collecting. As documented in the *Collecting Change/Changing Collections* report (Lee-Crossett 2018), active collecting (where the institution solicits donations or collects discarded materials from protest sites) is often held as the ideal. However, passive collecting (relying on activist-led donations) holds its advantages. Passive collecting is "responsive to communities' ideas and desires around what should be collected, rather than the organisation's priorities" (Lee-Crossett 2018, p. 5). Passive collecting works especially well in contexts where long-term relationships with communities and individuals have been established. Ultimately, by invoking museums and archives as *domains of protest memory*, we underscore the ways in which these memory institutions[5] showcase protest materials in ways that are "above all, archival. It relies entirely on the materiality of the trace, the immediacy of the recording, the visibility of the image" (Nora 1989, p. 13) to do its memory work.

Museums and Archives as Co-Creators of Protest Memory (see Table 3.1, Row 4)

This axis draws attention to a spectrum of archival production, collection and display strategies, generated through cultural institutions, which take place in real time and have participatory or collaborative aspects with visitors, partners and audiences. This is achieved through responding to live social issues, the commissioning of oral history accounts of recent protest and creating new mnemonic encounters through placing established collections in dialogue with contemporary social issues and campaigns. Under the axis of museums and archives as *co-creators of protest memory* (axis 4), cultural institutions are actively pursuing donations of protest materials, rather than waiting for them. This constitutes a key technique of rapid response collecting and curation, as we will explore in Chapter 4.

This axis spotlights emerging institutional work on 'co-creation' and 'co-production'.[6] As Jenny Rock and colleagues note, "Although repositioning museums from being 'open to the public' to becoming public oriented and co-produced has been long suggested, its enactment has been slow" (Rock et al 2018, p. 545). From a business and marketing context, co-creation refers to value creation between brands and customers. This includes the ability of customers to co-create personalised experiences (Holdgaard and Klastrup 2014, p. 192). In museum settings, co-creation pertains to "processes in which users are involved in creating new material that might or might not make use of memory materials already in the collection" (Marselis 2011, p. 85). This leads us to consider how museums and archives are actively working with audiences, communities, activists and users to co-create or co-produce protest memories.

To further understand how co-creation takes place in museum and heritage settings, we draw on Nina Simon's (2010) models of *contributions, collaborations, co-creations* and *hosted* activities, as a continuum of participation between cultural institutions and audiences. While we use the umbrella term 'co-creation' to name our axis, Simon's continuum provides a lens to think further about the extent and forms of such collaborative work. It should be noted that these models of participation can co-exist in the same project, and there is no intrinsic benefit or preference of more participation or collaboration with external partners; each project should respond to its own needs, resources and aims. In understanding and evaluating such projects, it is also important to attend to "where in the process external parties are involved and the degree to which the activity is shared between museum staff and external parties" (Davies 2010, p. 307). In what follows, we ground discussions of these participatory models through real-world examples drawn from the *Afterlives of Protest Research Network* partner, the People's History Museum (PHM).

In the model of audience *contribution*, visitors are solicited to provide objects or actions within an institutionally directed process. We find this at work in the audience-facing aspects of the exhibition *Never Going Underground: The Fight for LGBT+ Rights* (2017) at the People's History Museum, Manchester, UK. This exhibition presented documentary heritage of UK queer activism past and present.[7] Audience members were invited to add their perspectives and experiences to texts and spaces already set out in the exhibition, such as adding terms to a wall glossary, leaving messages for lost loved ones in an area for reflection, and contributing responses to the museum's provocation on the future of LGBTIQ+ rights (O'Donnell 2020). Moving up the scale of participation, in *collaborative* projects, visitors are invited to serve as active partners in the creation of institutional projects. This indicates a stronger degree of audience participation and autonomy, but the projects are still originated and ultimately controlled by the institution. The People's History Museum demonstrates this technique with their Protest Lab (2019), an open space within the *Disrupt? Peterloo and Protest* exhibition (introduced in Chapter 1), curated by Programme Officer Michael Powell. The Protest Lab aimed to connect the 200-year commemoration of the Peterloo Massacre with present-day activism, enacting a multidirectional protest memory orientation. The Protest Lab issued an open call for objects and invited donors to write their own label (or provide a spoken label) and supply further images, to tell their stories of protest and creative citizenship. The space started as a blank canvas on the launch of *Disrupt?* And slowly became populated with objects from visitors and local residents over the year. Objects ranged from climate change inspired parking tickets that local primary school children place on their parents' cars to encourage them to switch off their engines during the school pick up, to an anonymous fabric patch left by a participant involved in the pro-democracy Umbrella Movement in Hong Kong.[8]

With more autonomy and engagement, *co-created* projects see community members and external partners work together with institutional staff members from the outset to define the project's goals and to generate the programme or exhibit based on community interests. We see this at play in the 2020 exhibition theme of Migration at the People's History Museum, co-created by the Community Programme Team made up of seven individuals with lives shaped by migration. Working with PHM staff, the Community Programme Team re-examined and re-interpreted how migration was presented in the permanent exhibitions.

This gallery takeover generated new exhibits, digital installations and artistic responses.[9] Finally, in *hosted* interactions the institution turns over a portion of its facilities or resources to present programmes and exhibitions developed and implemented by public groups. Over 2023–2024, the People's History Museum is showcasing community-developed small exhibitions exploring the history of disabled people's rights and activism, to supplement their main exhibition and programming on the theme of disability rights activism. The PHM offers space, equipment, advice and funding, and require only a simple expression of interest via a short email, video message or sound recording to be considered.[10] Hosted projects allow participants to use institutions to satisfy their own needs with minimal institutional involvement, and, we add, could open up vibrant new channels for sourcing little known and undocumented protest memories.

Museums and Archives as Protectors, Carers and Innovators of Protest Memory (see Table 3.1, Row 5)

It is a truism to say that institutional memory workers care for collections. Caring for historical materials for posterity is a central task of the professional archivist, and the etymology of the term curator is drawn from the Latin 'to take care of'. Through the axis of the museum and archive as *protector, carer and innovator of protest memory* (axis 5), we attend to a set of practices that radically revisit the idea of care. Not only in terms of how care is undertaken for artefacts and objects, but also in terms of how care is extended to protest cultures and ideas, and to activists and wider communities. This radical understanding of care resonates with the paradigm shift within the museum sector from being "institutions concerned with the collection and care of historic objects, to institutions concerned with the lives of their visitors and their role in the betterment of society" (Wood and Cole 2019, p. 37). We recognise care as a form of social work and relationality that has long been devalued within patriarchal, capitalist and neoliberal governance. As a generative political ideal, care draws attention to the role of social capacity and interdependencies in "nurturing…all that is necessary for the welfare and flourishing of life" (Care Collective 2020, p. 5).[11] We emphasise that cultural memory has a role to play in this flourishing, as protest memories of social justice, democracy and liberation struggles exemplify the kinds of ideals and worlds worth caring for.

The heightened role of protector and carer of protest memory is well illustrated in the work of museum and archive professionals in Ukraine during the ongoing Russian invasion from February 2022. Alongside coordinated efforts from the international museums sector to aid Ukraine following the targeting of cultural and heritage institutions during the invasion,[12] the protection of protest memory and collections domestically demonstrates the risks that heritage professionals can assume. One such collection is the 4000 objects that constitute the Maidan Museum. This collection comprises of homemade flags, protest banners, hand-decorated tents, molotov cocktails and purloined police shields that were used by protesters in 2014 to defend themselves in protest camps in the Maidan Square in Kyiv, against state security forces, in the revolution that ousted the Putin-friendly government. At the time of writing, these objects are held in a secret location. As the curator Ihor Poshyvailo, who was instrumental in setting up the Maidan collection in 2014 and is currently collecting from Ukrainian resistance in 2022, explained to the *Guardian*: "Putin is very open in his desire to destroy the revolution of Maidan and therefore the museum is likely to be No 1 on the list to be liquidated. We know there is a list held by Russian occupiers as to who should be imprisoned first. They will look for military people, politicians, civil activists, but they will also look for cultural workers, especially those like us, who use culture to tell the story of Ukrainian nationhood" (Basciano 2022).[13] In this example, we see museum professionals safeguarding protest histories as *memory activists*, operating both within and outside of dangerous state attention, and with great risks to themselves.

Outside the heightened circumstances of conflict and war, this axis of innovation and care can also be seen at work in actions that subvert conventional professional approaches to artefacts, collections and exhibitions. During an expert workshop of the *Afterlives of Protest Research Network*, Stefan Dickers, Special Collections and Archives Manager at Bishopsgate Institute (BI), London, introduced the ways in which the archive can perform not as a repository of 'dead memory', as is the fear of many activists and practitioners (see Chapters 2, 4 and 5), but as a "living archive". As Dickers (2019) recounts, "We do a lot of live archiving, and this really upsets a lot of archive colleagues I have. A lot of the current protest stuff we take in, we allow groups to take it back out again, and some archivists can't get their head around this". These actions transform the institutional archive into an action-based protest resource where activists borrow their accessioned materials for ongoing campaigns, and then return them. Such archival activism is not without its risks. As Dickers told us, this can lead to preservation issues, or what he affectionately calls the "duct tape wars". Giving the example of environmental activists re-borrowing campaign materials such as posters, these artefacts were then affixed to surfaces with duct tape and oil-based blue tack, creating damage. In response, the BI archivists prepared a long note on which materials could be used, "which they now use all the time, which is wonderful". For Dickers, this type of institutional archival activism is part of celebrating archives: "Stuff given to you is given to you to be alive, to be out there. Every way I can possibly do it, it is about getting the archives out, getting them used, getting them looked at". For Dickers, what makes a radical archive is not just its contents, but its practices.

Rethinking the role of media and objects in protest memory generation is also central to understanding innovation. Attending to a people's history of art and design from below, the V&A exhibition *Disobedient Objects* (2014–2015), curated by Catherine Flood and Gavin Grindon, is exemplary in how to work *with* activists to produce an exhibition *for* activists and general audiences. Starting with the fact that memories "can cohere around objects in unpredictable ways" (Cvetkovich 2003, p. 242), Flood and Grindon subverted conventional curatorial practices to better represent a protest memory ethos within an institutional space. This ethos aims to embody activist practices, not just to represent them 'objectively' through the museum-eye.[14] Collecting together global activist ephemera and protest objects, spanning barricades, inflatables, puppets, tents, shields, banners, stencils and more, from the late 1970s to the present, Flood and Grindon adopted an innovative curatorial strategy that emphasised how activist cultures work. As the curators expressed, activism is full of polyvocal interpretations, lived experiences, networks and idiosyncratic trajectories (Flood and Grindon 2014). Rather than operationalising the curatorial power of the art museum and their own status as curators, Flood and Grindon provided two labels for each exhibit: one from themselves as curators, the other from the activist lenders who had *used or made* the protest objects being exhibited, therefore instructing the viewer about the object's social life.

The *Disobedient Objects* exhibition also drew on the museum's resources to distribute a series of free digital downloads instructing readers on how to make protest items (the guidance for creating a tear gas mask from a plastic bottle was subsequently used by several international protest movements; this provides a compelling example of the museum as an *agent of protest*). As Steve Lyons (2018, p. 5) noted in his erudite analysis of the exhibition, these bold curatorial practices "locked the museum into a feedback loop of global unrest—from protest to museum to protest". This co-produced the museum "as a potential resource for activist struggle".

Other techniques by the *Disobedient Objects* curators that embedded a protest memory ethos within the institution included pursuing small sponsors for the exhibition instead of one large corporate sponsor (mindful of *protest against the museum* in terms of arts sponsorship); collaborating on design decisions in consultation with activist communities; leaving objects open and accessible for visitors to photograph and touch; and staging a series of activist-led talks and workshops in the gallery space. Notably, the activist-practitioner stance behind this exhibition relied on subterfuge at times. As Lyons recounts: "this involved both withholding important pieces of information from V&A administration and describing their curatorial objectives in very different ways to different people", such as using the liberal ideals and curatorial language employed by the V&A to promote its work as an inclusive and accessible public institution, for internal and press communications (2018, p. 20). Grindon also prepared a "very vague talk about contemporary design" for the Board of Trustees, composed of London business leaders and conservative politicians appointed by the UK Prime Minister, to which a trustee fell asleep during the presentation and the exhibition proposal was approved without fuss (2018, p. 22). The most provocative objects in the exhibition, likely to cause public outrage as they could be read (uncritically) as 'promoting violent protest', were deliberately withheld from the museum administration until the objects were installed. In sum, Flood and Grindon reworked "the V&A's established conventions of exhibition, display, and fundraising" to generate a "model for disobedient curating" more broadly (2018, pp. 3, 24).

CONCLUSION

In generating this chapter's analytical framework, we have set forth a contextualising overview of key relations between protest, memory, museums and archives in the contemporary moment. This overview has generated a snapshot of the socio-cultural-economic and political relations in which museums, archives and activists engage with each other (directly or indirectly). In collating this framework, we remain mindful of the demands and pressures placed upon organisational and heritage actors in diverse contexts, and how cultural workers and artists are increasingly entering into the contested fray of protest memory.

This chapter has demonstrated that established museums and archives not only showcase the cultural legacies of protest from a historic and commemorative angle, but are increasingly becoming active intermediaries in the collection, shaping and support of protest actions in the here and now. Identifying five key axes of protest memory as they are produced within the GLAM sector, we have examined how museums and archives utilise a range of dynamics, techniques and practices to operate as (i) sites of protest, (ii) agents of protest, (iii) domains of protest memory, (iv) co-creators of protest memory and (v) protectors, carers and innovators of protest memory. Departing from the long-entrenched myth of 'political neutrality', an increasing number of memory institutions are boldly stepping into a new curatorial activist position: advocating on social and political issues, collecting protest materials and memories as they happen in real time, sharing resources and institutional space with activist groups to support community initiatives and generating networks of connection between protest past, present and future.

As sites of protest, we have joined our voices with other scholars to call on cultural institutions to create robust archives of protest which happen within their walls, and to consider future exhibitions engaging with these histories. As agents of protest, we have noted how museums have extended their social function into advocacy and civil resistance, taking on a more political role (again, we hope these activities are fully documented and archived to tell more complicated histories of the cultural sector and its role in society). Within our framework, we then took a closer look at how museums and archives have been engaging with protest memory as a theme, method and as an orientation. When operating as domains of protest memory, expertise and authority is kept within the actions of museum and archive professionals, and operating practices and display techniques continue to operate much in the same vein. As co-creators of protest memory, museums and archives look to distribute, share or decentre their expertise, working more closely with audiences, beneficiaries, artists and activists and introducing techniques of co-production within their focus on protest and protest memories. As protectors, carers and innovators of protest memory, museum and archival professionals explore radical new practices which challenge traditional working practices, and which may carry professional and personal risks. Taken together, this contentious memory work is emergent, uneven and conditioned by institutional and administrative scope, context and governance. While we advocate for archives and museums to engage in protest memory work within their institutions as part of their commitment towards knowledge-building and the protection of diversity, we recognise the limits that can be placed on such initiatives: not least with issues of funding, board approval and the political conditions in which museums and archives operate. We will continue to explore the dynamics and axes of our protest memory framework with more depth in the following case study chapters and in our final chapter reflections.

NOTES

1. Decolonize This Place (DTP) is a museum-oriented social movement, founded in New York in 2016. Its mission statement posits that "DTP resists and unsettles settler colonial structures in our cities as it builds movement infrastructure of care and solidarity...The university, museum, and city are sites of struggles and organizing. They are sites of refusal, sabotage, infrastructure, sanctuary, play, exit. Let them be sites of training in the practice of freedom" (https://decolonizethisplace.org). DTP actions have targeted the Whitney Museum, Metropolitan Museum of Art, American Museum of Natural History, among others, on issues related to indigenous recognition, colonial display strategies and the capitalist make up of museum boards.
2. After a six-year creative disobedience campaign by Liberate Tate (2010–2016), BP announced it was ending its twenty-six-year arts sponsorship of Tate in 2017.
3. The Museum of London articulated their position in a 2020 press release following BLM protests, issued on the day of the removal of the statue: "Robert Milligan was a prominent British Slave trader who, by the time of his death in 1809, owned 2 sugar plantations and 526 slaves in Jamaica...The Museum of London recognises that the monument is part of the ongoing problematic regime of white-washing history, which disregards the pain of those who are still wrestling with the

remnants of the crimes Milligan committed against humanity. At the Museum of London we stand against upholding structures that reproduce violence" (https://www.museumoflondon.org.uk/news-room/press-releases/robert-milligan-statue-statement).

4. Following the statue's removal, Tower Hamlets (the local authority), Canal and River Trust (the landowners) and the Museum of London Docklands formed a consortium with local communities to discuss possible next actions. A consultation found that 76% of people were in favour of the statue being presented in an exhibition. 43% believed it should be moved into storage at the museum and 15% said it should be kept permanently out of public view. Those in favour of keeping the statue on display suggested that it be exhibited with context about Milligan's involvement in the creation of the docks, his links to the slave trade and the recent Black Lives Matter movement (https://canalrivertrust.org.uk/refresh/media/thumbnail/45635-robert-milligan-detailed-project-report.pdf).

5. Museums and archives are not just cultural institutions, but also memory institutions. We note that scholars have critiqued the overarching concept of 'memory institutions' for its glossing of the aims, operating procedures, and historical development of distinct organisations. This includes "domain-specific approaches to the cataloguing, description, interpretation and deployment of collections", where provenance is the organising principle of archives, and narrative interpretation and contextualisation the organising principle of museums (Robinson 2012, p. 414). We use the term 'memory institution' here as it provides a lens for thinking through techniques of protest memory production and securitisation on an *institutional, meta-level*, as well as attending to the work of archivists and museum practitioners on an *individual, agentic level*. Our approach examines emergent, institutional and practitioner-based memory work that is pushing against sector and domain standards and expectations, while linking protest memory work to institutional creativity.

6. Co-creation, co-curation, collaboration, community involvement, co-design and co-production are often used synonymously. Co-production refers to how the consumers or end users of a product or service, co-produce the product or service with the resource holders, in governance, planning, design and/or implementation.

7. *Never Going Underground: The Fight for LGBT+ Rights* took place at the People's History Museum (PHM), Manchester, UK, 25 February–3 September 2017, funded by the National Lottery Heritage Fund. The exhibition marked the 50th anniversary of the 1967 Sexual Offences Act, which started the process to decriminalise homosexuality. The exhibition was co-produced with a team of nine Community Curators. It generated an award-winning major exhibition, three community exhibitions, a family-friendly public programme and a schools learning programme (https://www.heritagefund.org.uk/projects/never-going-underground-fight-lgbt-rights).

8. For a discussion of PHM's Protest Lab (2019) see https://phm.org.uk/blogposts/protest-lab-and-collecting-the-contemporary.

9. *Migration: A Human Story* ran between 25 August 2021 and 30 June 2022 at the PHM, supported by the Art Fund and the Joseph Rowntree Charitable Trust (https://phm.org.uk/programme/migration).

10. The PHM will host community exhibitions during 2023–2024 to support the main exhibition on disability activism, *Nothing About Us Without Us*. Policy guidelines state that community exhibitions must be accessible in terms of physical and intellectual access. The museum does not display items that are dangerous to the public (blades, live creatures, strobe lights, naked flames), potential health hazards (food and drink, nuts and seeds), items too large or heavy to carry into the building, or deemed to show hostility towards individuals or groups, including those with protected characteristics and those facing persecution (https://phm.org.uk/collaborations/nothing-about-us-without-us-community-exhibitions).

11. Murawski (2021, pp. 99–112) discusses *self-care* practices as essential for museum workers who labour to transform cultural institutions into healing justice organisations.

12. https://www.ne-mo.org/advocacy/our-advocacy-work/museums-support-ukraine.html.

13. Russian missiles hit the hometown of the Ukrainian Eurovision contestants, moments before the artists took to the stage at the Liverpool Arena for their Grand Final performance, 13 May 2023.

14. Museums have historically operated through gendered, classed and racialised visibility regimes to enact civic rituals and 'civic ways of seeing'. These practices instruct visitors in normative ideals and

behaviours. As Tony Bennett contends: "the terms in which questions of 'civic seeing' are now posed typically stress the need for exhibitions to be arranged so as to allow multiple possibilities in terms of how they are both seen and interpreted. The demands of indigenous peoples, of diaspora community and minority ethnic groups…of women, and of minority sexualities for recognition within the museum space have thrown into high relief the socially marked nature of the supposedly universal, singular points of view museums had earlier constructed" (2006, p. 278).

References

Basciano, O. 2022. 'We Collect Symbols of the Resistance': The Ukrainian Museum Working Through the War. *Guardian*, May 19. Available: https://www.theguardian.com/culture/2022/may/19/ukraine-maidan-museum-objects-ihor-poshyvailo-kyiv-cockerel. Accessed 9 Oct 2022.

Bennett, T. 2006. Civic Seeing: Museums and the Organization of Vision. In *A Companion to Museum Studies*, ed. S. Macdonald, 263–281. Oxford: Blackwell.

Collective, Care. 2020. *The Care Manifesto: The Politics of Interdependence*. London: Verso.

Cooper, S. 1987. The Politics of Protest Collections: Developing Social Action Archives. *Provenance* 5: 1. Available: https://digitalcommons.kennesaw.edu/provenance/vol5/iss1/3. Accessed 9 Oct 2022.

Cvetkovich, A. 2003. *An Archive of Feelings: Trauma, Sexuality, and Lesbian Public Cultures*. Durham: Duke University Press.

Davies, S.M. 2010. The Co-production of Temporary Museum Exhibitions. *Museum Management and Curatorship* 25 (3): 305–321.

Dickers, S. 2019. Roundtable Talk: Future Directions—Activist Museums Panel. *Curating Protest Memory Expert Workshop*, March 28. King's College London.

Flinn, A. 2011. Archival Activism: Independent and Community-Led Archives, Radical Public History and the Heritage Professions. *InterActions: UCLA Journal of Education and Information Studies* 7: 2. Available: https://doi.org/10.5070/D472000699. Accessed 9 Oct 2022.

Flood, C., and G. Grindon. 2014. Introduction. In *Disobedient Objects*, ed. C. Flood and G. Grindon, 6–25. London: V&A Publishing.

Holdgaard, N., and L. Klastrup. 2014. Between Control and Creativity: Challenging Co-creation and Social Media Use in a Museum Context. *Digital Creativity* 25 (3): 190–202.

Hopper, J. 2012. Naples Museum Director Begins Burning Art to Protest at Lack of Funding. *Guardian*, April 18. Available: https://www.theguardian.com/world/2012/apr/18/naples-casoria-museum-burning-art-protest. Accessed 9 Oct 2022.

Hoyer, J., and N. Almeida. 2021. *The Social Movement Archive*. Sacramento: Litwin Books.

Janes, R.R., and R. Sandell, eds. 2019. *Museum Activism*. London: Routledge.

Jones, J. 2018. 'Joyless in the Extreme'—I Object: Ian Hislop's Search for Dissent Review. *Guardian*, September 4. Available: https://www.theguardian.com/artanddesign/2018/sep/04/i-object-ian-hislop-search-for-dissent-review-british-museum. Accessed 9 Oct 2022.

Just Stop Oil. 2023. Statement on the Arrest of Just Stop Oil Supporters at Coventry Museum. *Just Stop Oil* [website], April 10. Available: https://juststopoil.org/2023/04/10/statement-on-the-arrest-of-just-stop-oil-supporters-at-coventry-museum. Accessed 10 July 2023.

Kavanagh, J. 2019. *Contemporary Collecting Toolkit*. Available: https://museumdevelopmentnorthwest.files.wordpress.com/2019/07/mdnw_contemporarycollectingtoolkit_july2019.pdf. Accessed 9 Oct 2022.

Lee-Crossett, K. 2018. *Collecting Change/Changing Collections*. Available: https://heritage-futures.org/collecting-changechanging-collections-report-goals-challenges-contemporary-collecting. Accessed 9 Oct 2022.

Lyons, S. 2018. Disobedient Objects: Towards a Museum Insurgency. *Journal of Curatorial Studies* 7 (1): 2–31.

MacLeod, S. 2007. Civil Disobedience and Political Agitation: The Art Museum as a Site of Protest in the Early Twentieth Century. *Museum and Society* 5 (1): 44–57.

Marselis, R. 2011. Digitising Migration Heritage: A Case Study of a Minority Museum. *MedieKultur. Journal of Media and Communication Research* 27 (50): 84–99.

McGreevy, N. 2022. In a Day-Long Protest, Dutch Museums Transform into Gyms, Nail Salons and Barber Shops. *Smithsonian Magazine*, January 25. Available: https://www.smithsonianmag.com/smart-news/dutch-museums-protest-covid-omicron-restrictions-180979442. Accessed 9 Oct 2022.

Murawski, M. 2021. *Museums as Agents of Change: A Guide to Becoming a Changemaker*. Lanham: Rowman & Littlefield.

Nora, P. 1989. Between Memory and History: Les Lieux de Mémoire. *Representations* 26: 7–24.

O'Donnell, C. 2020. Never Going Underground: Community Coproduction and the Story of LGBTQ+ Rights. In *Museums, Sexuality, and Gender Activism*, ed. J.G. Adair and A.K. Levin, 219–230. London: Routledge.

Raicovich, L. 2021. *Culture Strike: Art and Museum in an Age of Protest*. London: Verso.

Reed, T.V. 2019. *The Art of Protest: Culture and Activism from the Civil Rights Movement to the Present*, 2nd ed. Minneapolis: University of Minnesota Press.

Rees, S. 2019. Performative Objects. Panel—Protest Objects and Rapid Response Collecting. *Curating Protest Memory Expert Workshop*, March 28. King's College London.

Robertson, K. 2019. *Tear Gas Epiphanies: Protest, Culture, Museums*. Montreal: McGill-Queen's University Press.

Robinson, H. 2012. Remembering Things Differently: Museums, Libraries and Archives as Memory Institutions and the Implications for Convergence. *Museum Management and Curatorship* 27 (4): 413–429.

Rock, J., M. McGuire, and A. Rogers. 2018. Multidisciplinary Perspectives on Co-creation. *Science Communication* 40 (4): 541–552.

Simon, N. 2010. *The Participatory Museum*. Available: https://participatorymuseum.org. Accessed 9 Oct 2022.

Stapley-Brown, V. 2017. US Museums Challenge Trump's Immigration Ban in Court. *The Art Newspaper*, September 22. Available: https://www.theartnewspaper.com/2017/09/22/us-museums-challenge-trumps-immigration-ban-in-court. Accessed 9 Oct 2022.

Williams, M.E. 2017. A Noble Balancing Act: Museums, Political Activism and Protest Art. *Museum International* 69 (3–4): 66–75.

Wood, E., and S. Cole. 2019. Growing an Activist Museum Professional. In *Museum Activism*, ed. R.R. Janes and R. Sandell, 36–46. London: Routledge.

CHAPTER 4

Rapid Response Collecting

Abstract Centring the transnational Women's March (2017) that protested the first day in office of US President Donald Trump, this chapter examines the role of contemporary, cause-based collecting in museums and archives. Drawing on interviews with practitioners at the Bishopsgate Institute (London), People's History Museum (Manchester) and Victoria and Albert Museum (London), this case study examines the institutional processes behind collecting and curatorial efforts, including the important role of social media. We examine the cultural value that memory institutions deemed the protests to hold, what material culture was collected and how the Women's March was put into dialogue with historic protest to generate new protest memories. Through the case of the Women's March, we demonstrate the sped-up commemorative and documentary rhythms of contemporary protest cultures, and how memory is being conceived prospectively. We further attend to the presence (and lack) of intersectionality in the archive and assess public debates surrounding national museums engaging with activist cultures. Finally, we explore how museum and archive staff navigate self-reflexive evaluations of institutional (memory) activism.

Keywords Women's March · Pussyhat · Contemporary collecting · Intersectionality · Prospective memory

© The Author(s), under exclusive license to Springer Nature   81
Switzerland AG 2024
R. Chidgey and J. Garde-Hansen, *Museums, Archives and Protest Memory*, Palgrave Macmillan Memory Studies,
https://doi.org/10.1007/978-3-031-44478-4_4

Introduction: The Women's March and Prospective Memory

Dismayed by the electoral college defeat of Hillary Rodham Clinton on 8 November 2016, feminists quickly mobilised over social media to organise a mass protest to mark Donald Trump's first day in office as the 45th President of the United States.[1] Trump's campaign rhetoric was saturated with racist, misogynist and ableist speech acts and policies, in which his "strategies of deportation, walls, and internal violence" sought to bolster and "protect a threatened white masculinity which is portrayed as both victim and victor" (Gökariksel and Smith 2017, p. 628).[2] Based on eight principles of unity, the Women's March on Washington was coordinated as a single day of action on 21 January 2017 in response to the dangers the Trump administration posed to human rights, but it did not end there.[3] The organisers were clear from the start that the intention was to build a movement, not a moment, and that the march was the beginning of a mass-mobilisation of democratic and civic engagement. Many heeded this call. In an act of extraordinary solidarity, Women's Marches took place in 82 countries, across all seven continents, and with the participation of over 5 million people. As Heaney, a political scientist, noted: "No president in recent memory has faced protests from so many different directions at once" (2018, p. 43).

What remains further notable about these protest events is the central role of memory, commemoration and archival work that unfolded alongside. There was a shared understanding that the Women's March would be historically significant, and that *memories in activism* were required to be built from the grassroots in cooperation with heritage and cultural institutions. With this strategic aim, Danielle Russell and Katrina Vandeven, two professional archivists, spearheaded the Women's March on Washington Archive Project (WMOWAP), using the affordances of the commercial platform Facebook to enact archival activism. In their words, a living archive of activist oral histories and documentation surrounding the Women's March was urgently required, "given the centuries long archival silence in respect to women's interaction with the state, which has in turn de-legitimized their history as political actors".[4]

Discourses of memory were also at the heart of the *Pussyhat Project*. This viral arts advocacy project encouraged protesters to make use of a free design to create protest hats and to create a "sea of pink" as a strong statement of solidarity for women's rights, as we will come to discuss.

The *Pussyhat Project* launched on 22 November 2016, two months ahead of Trump's inauguration. Its visual manifesto orientated the project "in *anticipation* and *commemoration* of the Women's March on Washington DC" (Fig. 4.1, emphasis added), notably evoking memory *before* the first protest action had even taken place.

These mnemonic actions challenge common-sense understandings of memory and commemoration as happening *after* an event, as something that is backward-looking. Within digitally connective mediascapes, and with memory-savvy activists and archivists at the helm, memory practices are instead being launched *prospectively*, in anticipation of protest and its historic significance. These examples highlight the accelerated

Fig. 4.1 Visual manifesto for *The Pussyhat Project Knit Pattern*. Artwork Aurora Lady, 2016. Courtesy of Jayna Zweiman

temporalities of collecting, archiving and memorialising activism within digital mediascapes. Such high-speed mnemonic rhythms at the grass-roots find their companion in the arts and heritage sector methodology of 'rapid response collecting'. In response to significant events locally and (trans)nationally, this method prompts institutions to "collect the ephemeral and the momentous that might be difficult to acquire once the phenomenon is over" (Debono 2021, p. 180).[5] Or, as one journalist put it, to "get a head start on history" (Marshall 2018).

This chapter seeks to understand how UK collecting organisations approached rapid response collecting of the Women's March. We examine what cultural value these organisations deemed the protests to hold, what material culture was collected and how the Women's March was put into dialogue with historic protest to generate new digital and embodied protest memories. Spotlighting three UK collecting institutions, we draw on interviews held in the summer of 2017 with practitioners from the Bishopsgate Institute (London), People's History Museum (Manchester) and the Victoria and Albert Museum (London).[6] These interviews are complemented with data drawn from contemporaneous social media and news reports to better contextualise public and journalistic responses to the collecting initiatives.[7] In what follows, we examine the practices of co-creating and supporting protest memory in real time, including the techniques of care and innovation. We also explore some key challenges the cultural and heritage workers experienced when participating in this prospective form of protest memory management.

SOCIAL MEDIA, THE BISHOPSGATE INSTITUTE AND THE DECISION TO COLLECT

Social media played a heightened role in the Women's March media-memory-activism nexus, enabling activism and (professional) archivisation to meet at speed. We see this in the example of the Bishopsgate Institute (BI). Nicky Hilton, then Digital Archives Manager at the BI, attended the Women's March in London on 21 January 2017 in a personal capacity. That morning, at 9am, Hilton posted the following message from her Twitter account: "#womensmarchlondon. Make sure #Trump can't call this #fakenews. Send your placards&photos to @BishopsgateInst Protest Archive! DM [direct message] me for info". As we have noted in earlier chapters, and will evidence further in Chapter 5, the Bishopsgate Institute has garnered a strong reputation as a preeminent centre for documenting

activism and protest in the UK. As a memory institution it has cultivated excellent relations with activist donors. The BI is an archive and
public reading room based in the City of London, independently funded,
and with a history stretching back to 1895 as a site for public education.
Its extensive Special Collections and Archive documents activism, protest
and campaigning materials from the nineteenth century onwards, with a
particular focus on London campaigns. Part of the success of the BI in
collecting activist materials is its independent status and its commitment
to making a safe, welcoming and accessible space. As Hilton explained:

> we have some advantages because we're not connected to the council.
> We're not government funded. That makes us much more attractive...If
> you have been rallying against the government all your life, you're unlikely
> to donate to the British Library because they are government funded...if
> you have spent your life being a counter-narrative, you might not want to
> do that.

In addition, the size of the BI enables greater archival autonomy:
"We're a very small organisation. There's only 28 of us...It's very easy
to go and talk to our CEO. Generally the library is kind of autonomous
in that, as long as we don't bring in something that is hugely controversial
or enormous, we have a lot of freedom to collect what we want".

While the BI regularly collects contemporary protest materials, this
is usually done through approaching campaign organisations directly.
Hilton's tweet on the morning of the Women's March in 2017, enacted
a more distributed *co-creation of protest memory*, with its call to unknown
marchers, inviting them to donate placards and digital photographs.
In our interview, Hilton explained that this call for materials was not
pre-planned. She issued the Twitter call only after realising how large
the event was going to be. Stefan Dickers, the Special Collections and
Archives Manager at BI, also tweeted for donations via his personal
account. As Hilton explained, the uptake from donors was unusual: "we
had put out calls on Twitter before for other protests without much
success. We got the same faces we got anyway, the people who already
know us, who've already donated stuff to us, who've been protesting
for years and are seasoned protesters". While unsure about "what the
magic formula" was with the Women's March, Hilton suggested that the
personal, connective nature of the march (facilitated through the hashtag

#WhyIMarch) and the mainstream and social media attention it garnered were key factors in the success with donations.

There was certainly a public 'commemorative buzz' around the event. As part of the media-memory-activism nexus composed through connective media and hashtags, Hilton and Dickers' tweets were picked up by the ITN news agency. This fed into wider reporting from local and national media outlets, including *Time Out* and *The Independent*, the commercial women's magazines *The Stylist* and *Grazia*, and international publications such as the *Huffington Post*, the latter of which remediated tweets from museums and archives in the UK, US and Canada collecting from the Women's March.

As museum scholars have noted with regard to contemporary collecting, "the decision about when to collect is equally as significant as the decision about why, how and what to collect" (Salahu-Din 2019, p. 102). Archivists' engagement with social media, including using hashtags to enable protesters to see the donation calls in real time, was instrumental in generating a good response to archival efforts. Hilton reflected that the personal tweets (rather than institutional tweets, which received little engagement) connected to the highly individual nature of the march. She observed that the Women's March was qualitatively different from earlier protest marches the BI had collected from, such as the 2003 Stop the War marches against the Iraq war. The Women's March held no overarching focus, aim or demand beyond the eight principles of unity. In lieu of professionally printed signs and singular messages, the Women's March was characterised by a sea of handcrafted placards and witty, personal statements. The diversity of statements and protest aesthetics, according to Hilton, made the Women's March appear "like social media on the street...everyone was saying their own message". This led to a challenge from a collecting point of view, "because it's a lot of individuals and how do you capture all those voices, how do you make sure that all those people who were there are heard rather than just the ones the mainstream media went for, which was a lot of Pussyhats".[8]

In the days following the Women's March in London, 48 people donated digital photos and artefacts to the BI, including 22 physical placards. Hilton noted this was a strong response. Many of the donors had seen the call on social media, or the call remediated in media outlets. It was typically their first time visiting the BI. Hilton noted that when receiving the donations, many marchers believed their protest materials would be on display immediately. Hilton clarified that the BI is an archive, not a museum: "We don't have anywhere where we could put [the photos and placards] securely. If we had a big cabinet, they would've been straight in there, but unfortunately, no". These materials were not destined for inert archival boxes, however. In the months following accession, the BI used Women's March materials in their adult education classes, archive tours and 'pop-up archives' to accompany talks (where, for example Women's March materials sat on a table next to women's suffrage materials; as Hilton notes, "people find it quite interesting, that connect between the two"). The BI also lent materials to museums for display.

Hilton then discussed the innovative strategies that she undertook on the level of record management, which we can view within the dynamic of archive as a *protector, carer and innovator of protest memory*. Hilton realised, after the first few donations were dropped off, that there was an opportunity to collect richer information than was required from the standard consent form for ephemeral items, such as personal details and copyright permission.[9] As she recalled:

> I suddenly thought it'd probably be really good to know why people were marching, because they were so personal. It was a bit of a learning curve. We'd not done this before [a spontaneous social media call for materials] and we didn't really know what to expect. Thereafter I just informally had a chat with people and said why did you march; who did you march with, you know. Tell me about this; why did you choose these words, and then wrote it down in the catalogue as what I call an archivist note. It's my interpretation of what they've said to me. I've tried to be quite clear that it isn't verbatim. It's what I gleaned from the conversation.

The highly creative and personal aspect of the Women's March is significant, as it forms the main impetus for capturing the personal stories behind the donations. As Hilton reflected, "It's not something in the archive profession [that you tend to do], that idea that you get a sense of the bodies behind the objects".

These archivist notes add value by capturing connections between donors and wider protest memories. For instance, we learn of a donor who was involved in an iconic 1970 protest event of the UK's women's liberation movement,[10] and a donor actively involved in contemporary trans* activism and queer cultural production (Fig. 4.2). The archivist notes also capture the personal reasons behind the speech acts presented on the hand-made signs (Fig. 4.3). One placard proclaims, "Middle Class and PROUD!". The donor positions this as a response to the 'silencing' of feminist activists from class-privileged backgrounds through the phrase 'check your privilege'. This necessarily raises important considerations of how racial and socio-economic class privilege is embodied and reflexively understood in feminist activist movements, and how intersectionality is being invoked, or absented.[11]

Another placard exclaims "All Lives Matter". As the donor explained, this referred to animal rights under Trump's administration. However, this speech act can be placed within a wider context of white appropriations of the Black Lives Matter slogan, which enacts a decentring of public debates about race and racism.[12] Hilton's archivist notes, made in *media res*, provide important information for future researchers to help them understand how the media-memory-activism nexus is being constructed, and to further understand the motivations, contentions and aims of individual protesters. That is, how social movement knowledge travels and is taken up.

Rather than producing a 'smooth' protest memory or over-emphasising the aesthetic qualities of the hand-made signs, these archivist notes invite further reflection and contextualisation. The examples above point to intra and cross-movement 'frictions' and 'borrowings', which are crucial to grapple with when approaching protest memory in its embodied complexity. Such data, scaffolded by a modest archival innovation at the level of a publicly accessible record of an exchange with donors, creates a starting point to address issues of intersectionality and memories of individual protest agents. Such database records provide evidence of how protest subjectivities and strategies are composed, how individuals see their place and values in wider political networks and gesture to what is being centred—and erased—through such forms of political speech acts.

Protest Signs, Preservation and Issues of 'Dead Memory' at the People's History Museum

The People's History Museum (PHM) is a national museum of democracy. Starting life in 1975 as the National Museum of Labour History in London, the institution moved to Manchester in 1988 and rebranded as the People's History Museum in 2002. It holds a collection of 60,000 objects designated of national importance and displays the largest number of trade union and political banners in the world. In 2022, the PHM

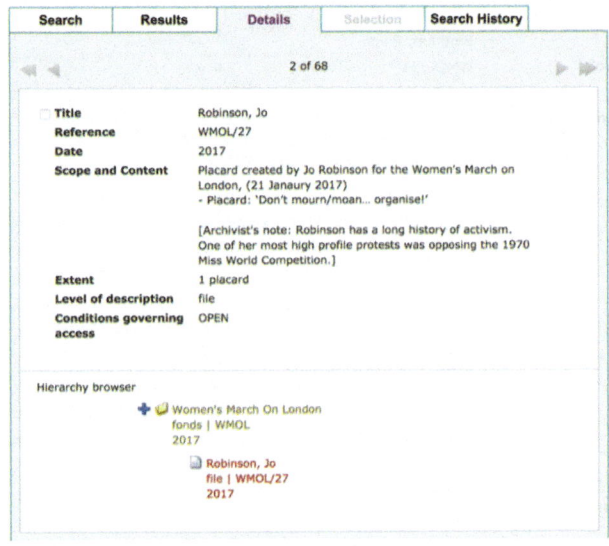

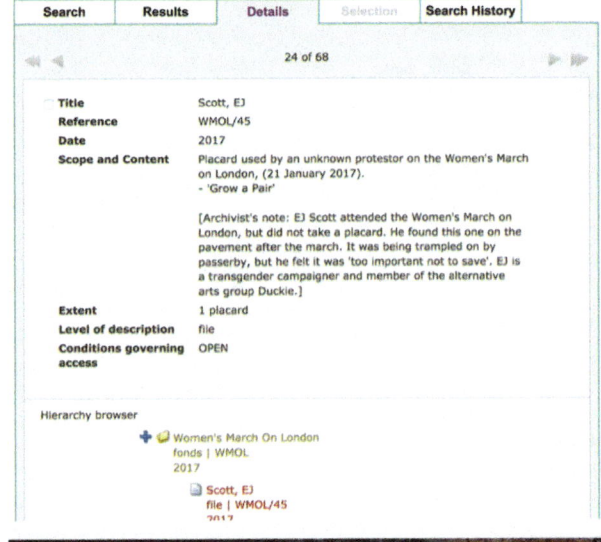

Fig. 4.2 Feminist, queer and trans* protest memories in the database record, 2017, Bishopsgate Institute

☐ Title	Banham, Pippa
Reference	WMOL/31
Date	2017
Scope and Content	Double-sided placard created and used by Pippa Banham at the Women's March on London (21 Janaury 2017). - Placard, 'Middle Class and PROUD! I Drive A Vulva', and 'Grab 'Em By The Policy'. [Archivist note: Banham is a member of the Suffolk Feminist Society, and contributor to the podcast Broad Agenda. She choose to highlight her 'middle class' credentials on the placard because as a white, educated women she is often told to 'check her privilege' and not to talk for other women. Banham feels very aware of the advantages she's had in her life, using them to inform her activism. She believes that a discussion about the need for multiple voices in the women's movement has been appropriated by those who protect the status quo and is now used as another way to silence and discredit politically active women.]
Extent	1 placard
Level of description	file
Conditions governing access	OPEN

☐ Title	Smith, Jane
Reference	WMOL/29
Date	2017
Scope and Content	Fabric tabard created by Jane Smith and worn on the Women's March on London, (21 Janaury 2017). - Love Trumps Hate...everytime...everywhere. All Lives Matter'. [Archivist's note: The tabard was made from an old pillowcase, with fleece sewn into the front to provide insulation. The wording was created with fabric paint and stitching. In the letter which accompanied the donation, Smith explained that she used the phrase, 'All Lives Matter', to highlight Trump's proposed policies regarding livestock farming (Smith was concerned that it would be a case of 'profit at the expense of animal welfare').]
Extent	1 tabard
Level of description	file
Conditions governing access	OPEN

Fig. 4.3 Tracing political standpoints and movement borrowings in the database records, 2017, Bishopsgate Institute

was shortlisted for the Art Fund Museum of the year, and in 2021 won the Activist Museum Award. The PHM is committed to highlighting struggles for equality by workers, activists, citizens and migrants.

Helen Antrobus, then Programme and Events Officer, issued the call for donations for the Women's March on 23 January 2017 (after the event), using the PHM's official Twitter account. The tweet had a good level of engagement from historians and activists, and the Museum Association remediated the call on their website. At the time the PHM was experiencing understaffing issues and had no contemporary collecting policies in place to collect from live protests. The tweet was something of a gamble—with Antrobus unsure of what the donor response would be. In actuality, the bulk of donations came from the Women's March Manchester co-organiser, Jen Langton-Sneyd, who rounded up discarded placards to bring to the PHM. The donations were accepted and discussed by the Acquisitions Committee in terms of what to keep.[13] The committee took into consideration storage and conservation issues, as well as opportunities for education and exhibitions. As Antrobus explained, "for some [signs] the conservation issues are quite problematic. When you're collecting ephemera, [activists] use things like tape, glue, all these kinds of things, which will break down and fail". The signs were made from a range of everyday materials: cardboard, felt tip pens, cellotape, bamboo poles and ribbon, with a quick decay time. Due to bad weather during the march, signs were also damp and had to be dried out; some were splattered with dirt and organic matter.

Beyond discarding signs with serious preservation concerns, the donations were evaluated for representativeness. Heritage professionals have noted several factors to help determine collection decisions: representativeness of a personal story, community or identity; resonance with media headlines and social trends or zeitgeists; effectiveness of storytelling (when materials represent experiences or emotions and help to put people back in the collection); and materials made in conversation with communities (Lee-Crossett 2018, pp. 4–5). The acquisition meeting viewed signs with hashtags favourably, as they enable the museum to "talk about social media and its relationship to protest", as Adam Jaffer, then Collections Officer, contextualised. Jaffer continued, "we chose a mixture of things that were very specific and things that we could use in other galleries on other issues", including a sign lampooning Trump (Fig. 4.4) earmarked for a PHM exhibition on political cartoons later that year. As Jaffer noted, this "is a pretty quick turnaround for a museum because usually things sit in store for years and then get in displays".

Copyright restrictions came into play when deciding which items to accession. Many of the protest signs were donated via a third-party (the Women's March Manchester co-organiser). The PHM did not have explicit permission from the individual protesters to transfer copyright and ownership, and the objects became orphan works.[14] As Jaffer explained, "we still don't really have the copyright of these objects. Like a lot of things in the collection we don't know who made them, they are just in our collection, and we will take the risk". The implication is that the signs can be displayed, but potential problems occur when the museum wishes to reproduce an image, as the signs are "cultural products [...] and copyright is a kind of professional etiquette that you want to credit people who produce stuff and it is a courtesy that their talent, their creativity gets recognised". Copyright issues also came into play when activists had

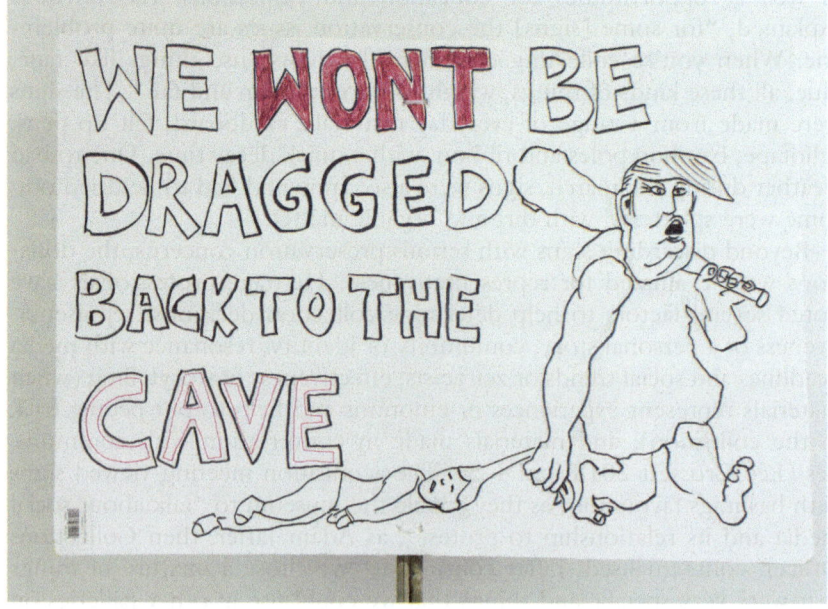

Fig. 4.4 Women's March Manchester protest sign, 2017. Creator unknown. Courtesy of the People's History Museum

remediated images from other sources. As Jaffer explained: "say someone had done a placard and they had got a picture off *Sky News* website of Donald Trump and stuck that on there. Now unless they manipulate for the purpose [of] satire [...] the copyright of the image remains with Sky". If protest signs included such third-party copyrighted material, it was not selected for acquisition to protect the institution from legal redress. Signs that were not selected were used by the learning team for their activities or disposed of following communication with the donor.

In terms of the PHM's positionality, the institution would have collected pro-Trump signs, had they been offered. As Antrobus contextualised, "[we] have to be very politically neutral". Jaffer continues: "it's important for us to say we're collecting an event that happened, whether we agree with it or not". Alongside discussing the decision-making process of what made it into the collection, during our interview, Antrobus and Jaffer also reflected on the implications of holding 'live protest objects' in the museum. Jaffer reflected on the materiality of protest cultures and sensitively expressed an ambivalence he held about protest objects entering institutional spaces: "Once it's in a museum it gets kind of neutralised...objects go to museums when they die". He continues: "these things had a life in the real world and now they are here and they're serving a different purpose, a much more passive purpose. They're not ritualistic, they're not protests...in a museum, which are essentially conservative institutions...its been recuperated". This echoes the concerns of the curators behind the V&A's exhibition *Disobedient Objects*, discussed in Chapter 3. From a memory perspective, it issues an important provocation that we will return to in Chapter 6. As Jaffer proposed: "It's not about the thing, it's about the social relationships", which leads us to consider innovative approaches to protest object collection and curation.

THE PINK PUSSYHAT: A CONTESTED DESIGN OBJECT FOR THE V&A MUSEUM

The pink Pussyhat, conceived by design architect Jayna Zweiman and screenwriter Krista Suh in Los Angeles in November 2016 in the run-up to the Women's March on Washington, became a key visual protest memory of the march.[15] Composed of a simple knitted or crocheted rectangle, folded in half and stitched at the edge to create 'cat ears' when placed on the head, the Pussyhat was designed as a protester-led strategy to create a powerful visual statement of solidarity for women's rights. For Zweiman and Suh the connotations of the hat were threefold. The 'pussy' connotations referenced the sexual assaults of Trump; Trump was caught on tape for *Access Hollywood* in 2005 discussing groping and "grabbing women by the pussy", a video of which made the rounds during the election campaign. Pink was selected as a colour to represent femininity, a socially marginalised and under-valued social relation. And the DIY nature of the hats represented a powerful form of "craftivism" (Black 2017), highlighting how traditionally 'feminine arts' such as knitting and crochet can be used for subversive purposes.

Many protesters heeded the call, making the Pussyhat Project one of history's largest advocacy art projects. In the short span of fifty-nine days, tens of thousands of hats were created, gifted and worn at Women's Marches around the globe. Such was the spectacle of this eye-catching pink protest object that journalists labelled them the "beloved icon" of the Women's March (Cascone 2017). However, such a statement of affection belies that many women of colour, non-binary and trans* people critiqued the Pussyhat for its association to female genitalia, arguing that not all women have vaginas, not all people with vaginas are women and not all vaginas are pink. Feminists further critiqued the Pussyhat with its 'cat ears', arguing the image was infantilising and a 'silly' design.[16]

On 13 February 2017, a Pussyhat entered the permanent collection of the Victoria and Albert Museum (V&A) as part of their Rapid Response Collecting activities.[17] The V&A is an institutional leader in rapid response collecting. It launched the Rapid Response Collecting gallery in 2014, before these artefacts were integrated into a suite of galleries dedicated to twentieth- and twenty-first-century design in 2021. Within the initial Rapid Response initiative, newsworthy, contemporary objects of design and manufacturing were acquired and put on display, with five showcases enabling twelve objects to be displayed at a time.[18] As Corinna Gardner, then Acting Keeper of the Design, Architecture and Digital Department of the V&A, explained in our interview:

> A museum for me is a place for debates, discussion. I very much feel that we have a responsibility to think about the here and now and to enable each other to think more broadly about how we each experience the world. Design objects allow us to focus on big and difficult questions around a material thing and this is a great starting point. These objects are nodes of

much larger systems. If we're able to look at the node we could open and unparcel and think about different perspectives on the world around us.

Thought-provoking items collected via the Rapid Response initiative include the world's first 3-D printed handgun (2013), a painted umbrella from the Hong Kong pro-democracy movement (2014), a refugee flag commissioned to support the first refugee team competing at the Olympic Games in Rio de Janeiro (2016), and a pulse oximeter to highlight systemic racism in the design of medical technologies (2022). For Gardner, the Pussyhat (2017) was a significant item to collect, not only as a handcrafted item emblematic of global Women's Marches and a key icon of solidarity, but because of its status as a *digital object*. This reading enhances our understanding of how contemporary design is enabled and distributed via digital technologies, and, in Gardner's words, "how digital culture is becoming material".

The open-source designs for the Pussyhat were posted on the project website www.pussyhatproject.com and circulated on social media and knitting sites via the hashtag #pussyhatproject, attracting an estimated 10,000 downloads in the run-up to the march. Crafters who could not attend the Women's March on Washington and beyond were invited to create a Pussyhat and gift it to a marcher with a personal note, the template of which was provided via the Pussyhat Project. By encouraging such gifts to be sent to the project organisers, who then distributed them at the Women's March on Washington, the idea was to create a platform for people to support women's rights and each other, and to create networks for future political activism (gifters had the option of including their contact details to start conversations with those who had worn their hats). For Zweiman and Suh, the Pussyhat Project constituted a social movement initiative and a "design intervention for social change".[19]

For the V&A curatorial team, the Pussyhat came into their orbit following Trump's inauguration and the significant media visibility the artefact had acquired. As Gardner recalls, the first step was asking: "is this [object] important enough in and of itself? My view is often that the object needs to have had a life in the world, a material consequence". The Pussyhat certainly had a heightened presence in the media-memory-activism nexus, with many images posted online of protesters of all ages donning the Pussyhat, the protest object gracing the front cover of *The New Yorker* and *Time* magazine, celebrities in Pussyhats sharing selfies to endorse the march, Pussyhats appearing on *Saturday Night Live* and the hats even appearing on the catwalk of Milan Fashion Week. Such was the popularity of this craftivism (albeit one that came to be perceived as white and cisgender centred),[20] that shortages of pink yarn were reported in the US in the run-up to the march (BBC 2017).

As part of their research, the curatorial team at the V&A conducted a social media poll to garner public interest in the potential acquisition.[21] Several hats were offered, which prompted further reflection in the team. As Gardner noted: "This is a challenge of the contemporary and also the multiple or the digital object, which I consider [the Pussyhat] to be, despite the fact it's made of wool". The proximity of the hat to its original source was an important factor for the final acquisition. After a successful approach to the creators of the Pussyhat Project, a hat knitted by project co-creator Jayna Zweiman and worn at the Washington, D.C. march was acquired. For Gardner, "that sense of provenance, that personal narrative, the context that this gives to the object is vitally important".[22] The acquisition comprised of the Pussyhat artefact, the Pussyhat Project knitting design pattern and a note from maker to wearer.

The artefacts entered the collection on 13 February 2017, a mere twenty-four days after the Women's March took place. The Rapid Response collection development strategy expedites the processes of paperwork and approval. A registered file is made on accession, which documents the correspondence surrounding the acquisition. For the exhibit (Fig. 4.3), the date when the object entered the collection is displayed, along with a central hook expressing the artefact's significance: "A knitting pattern that defied a president". The curators have around 150 words ("long by museum standards", Gardner notes) to articulate what the object is, why the museum acquired it and why it is important as a design object.[23] "Then we have what in museum language is known as the tombstone label, which is the who, how, what of the object. And with Rapid Response, at times when it's helpful or conducive, we include either a photograph or an ancillary object or some video footage". For the Pussyhat display, a press photograph of the Women's March on Washington was selected to demonstrate the actualisation of the "sea of pink" that the Pussyhat founders had envisioned (Fig. 4.5).[24]

The V&A press team selected International Women's Day (8th March) to announce the acquisition to the public, tacitly linking this protest object to wider feminist repertoires.[25] Gardner noted that while she

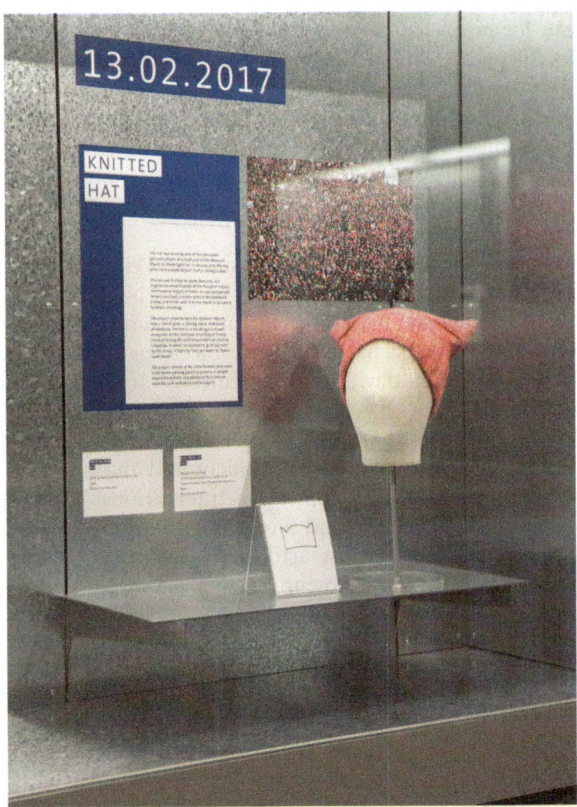

Fig. 4.5 Pussy Power Hat, by Jayna Zweiman, on display in the Rapid Response Gallery, Victoria and Albert Museum, London, 2017. Courtesy of ©Victoria and Albert Museum, London

didn't want "to orchestrate the activity of Rapid Response too much to follow [a] media agenda or calendar", there was a promotional benefit to coincide with "earmarked activity beyond the walls of the institution". As well as the press release, the acquisition was promoted via the museums' Facebook page. The social media activity on this post is instrumental for understanding public reactions to collecting contemporary protest materials, as indicated in the following anonymised replication of the Facebook comments the announcement received:

Poster 1: Yeah for pussy hat power!!

Poster 2: No. Just stop. You're the V&A for heavens sake.

Poster 3: Can you please elaborate on your comment? It is VERY unclear.

Poster 4: This is very political. All women do not agree with it. This is not the role of a museum to support one side or another.

Poster 5: Museums collect and display objects. There's no support implied. A large proportion of what's in Museums is 'political'. They wouldn't be very good museums otherwise.

Poster 4: No support implied? This is so insincere. Will the A&V [sic] buy something from Trump's women supports? [sic] No. One side and only one will be represented. I don't care, I'm not American, I'm not even for Trump, but this is partial. And this object has been presented here on the Women's rights day. Isn't that curious? It isn't insensere [sic], this is hypocritical.

Poster 6: Ffs [for fuck sake] it has cultural significance. It symbolizes a major cultural (and yes, political) movement and an important moment of reinvigorated activism. It is topical on International Women's Day, as the #DayWithoutAWoman[26] and women's strikes take place. I'm sure there'll be Trump and Rightist artifacts in museums. Today is about symbols of the women's movement.

There are four discourses at play in this social media exchange. The first is support for the museum for collecting contemporary cultural and political ephemera to capture an important historic moment ("it has cultural significance"). The second is that collecting from popular culture is 'beneath' the V&A as a design museum ("Just stop. You're the V&A for heavens sake"). As Gardner reflected in our interview, "[some] people were entirely outraged, that the museum that is the national collection of fashion and textiles has acquired [in their opinion] such an ugly object, or such a basic [artefact], into the collection". For Gardner, such views are tied up with perceptions of elitism; that the museum's purpose is to "earmark excellence". Instead, she suggests, the key premise of Rapid Response Collecting is that "each and every object is chosen on the basis of its ability to tell a story through its design".

The third discourse is that museums should refrain from being 'political' ("This is not the role of a museum to support one side or another"). Tied up with this statement is the assumption that an acquisition equates to political support, which raises difficult questions for collecting institutions.[27] Also underpinning this discourse is the belief in 'political neutrality' (as discussed in Chapter 2), which has considerable public and institutional sway, yet is challenged by one poster ("Museums collect and display objects. There's no support implied. A large proportion of what's in Museums is 'political'"). Gardner notes the V&A holds many objects of protest, so the Pussyhat is not unique in this regard. She also emphasised that "Rapid Response is not there to make you think in a particular way, it's to offer you the tools and to enable your imagination to set flight". Here Gardner cites the Vote Leave leaflet (2016) in the collection, drawn from 4.2 million printed and distributed during the UK Brexit campaign. This leaflet employed designs associated with the National Health Service [NHS] to invite (and mislead) readers to "Help protect your local hospital" by voting leave in the European Union Membership referendum. This artefact provides material evidence for how design has been utilised within the post-truth era of misinformation and 'fake news' (the latter term also used by Hilton in her tweet for donations from the Women's March, and reflective of the age of 'alternative facts' heightened within the Trump era and social media, see McIntyre 2018).

The fourth and final discourse is the sense that 'both sides of the story' should be represented, or will be represented in the GLAM sector at large ("Will the A&V [sic] buy something from Trump's women supports? [sic] No. One side and only one will be represented", "I'm sure there'll be Trump and rightist artifacts in museums"). We return to this point in Chapter 6 as we reflect on key challenges and risks that museum and archivist professionals face in the representation of contentious politics. Reflecting on these public views, Gardner raises a significant point with regard to her team's collection development policies:

> what it said on the Facebook feed is whether you're acquiring [Trump ephemera] as the counter-voice, and my view is that Rapid Response is that juxtaposition in direct terms. We didn't acquire a counterpoint to the Primark jeans that were collected in the immediate aftermath of the Rana Plaza factory [disaster, which claimed over a thousand lives of Bangladeshi garment workers as the eight-storey building collapsed]. The counterpoint is the broader context of the institution, our 2.5 million objects, but also the wider world around us. It's not about needing to be representative in those terms, that's not what the purpose of our activity is, or indeed why these designed objects are important to us.

CONCLUSION: INSTITUTIONAL ACTIVISM AND FEMINIST AFTERLIVES

This chapter has examined contemporary cause-based collecting surrounding the transnational Women's March. Through interviews with museum and archive professionals, we have explored a range of collecting decisions and processes. The impromptu act of an archivist attending the Women's March in London in a personal capacity and tweeting for donations for the Bishopsgate Institute in situ. The belated call from the People's History Museum that resulted in the co-organiser of the Women's March Manchester collecting discarded placards days after the event to donate. The curatorial processes of gaining a Pussyhat from the Women's March on Washington for the V&A Rapid Response Collecting gallery. Each one of these acts drew on the agency of individual cultural memory workers, were facilitated using commercial social media platforms, became remediated to wider publics through the media-memory-activism nexus, and which led to new audiences visiting the case study institutions.[28]

In the case of the People's History Museum, the encounter with the organiser of the Women's March in Manchester, Jen Langton-Sneyd, led to an ongoing collaboration. Langton-Sneyd continued to work with the PHM on the co-created centennial exhibition of the Representation of the People Act 1918, which enabled the first women to vote in the UK after fifty plus years of women's political agitation.[29] As Jaffer noted, "you can make those parallels between what happened in the past and today, which you'll find lots of museums do. It can bring subjects which are maybe a bit remote to people, up to date". Like the Bishopsgate Institute, the material culture of the women's suffrage movement was highlighted and put into conversation with the protest artefacts of the Women's March at the PHM. These encounters help create new imaginaries around dissent and foster multidirectional protest memories. This strategy also prompts us to think critically about what is being included and left out of the memorialisation of resistance.

Alongside detailing how audiences perceive the significance of contemporary cause-based collecting, this case study has sought to examine how institutional actors navigate the demands of collecting contentious or political objects, and what values and vibrancies they perceive these protest objects to have. With the rise of discourses of "museum activism" (Janes and Sandell 2019), it is pertinent to reflect on the ways in which professional memory workers understand and resonate with such claims. As discussed earlier, Antrobus and Jaffer saw their role as being "politically neutral" and open to collecting from opposing views within a particular protest event or movement. To contextualise, Antrobus made a comparison to the PHM having considerable anti-women's suffrage materials in their collections. On the issue of whether they saw themselves as activist archivists, or engaging in curatorial activism, the response from the interviewees was thoughtful. Hilton, as an archivist, argued that even if they were politically committed to transformational activism, "you can't be fully an activist" in an institution, as "you still have to present all voices or attempt to present all voices and be impartial in the way I present the information that's given to me". For Gardner, the issue was not activism, per se, but democratisation:

> Am I seeking to democratise the museum in the work I do? Absolutely yes. But that's because no institution that is publicly funded should not be for every person, and I'm deeply committed to that. Rapid Response is not a tool to do that specifically, it's not that I'm going to find objects that make the museum more democratic. It's about a broader reaching of design, and that speaking for a wider sector of society, the *every* person. We as institutions, and we specifically as an institution, need to be better at it.

Gardner continues: "That's about museums being open, being generous, having a sense that they don't have a monopoly on expertise". This recognition of shared authority, which decentres the expertise and viewpoint of the museum and archivist professional yet acknowledges them as the ultimate decision-maker, was a common perception among the responses. Gardner expressed a sentiment shared by other interviewees when she stated: "you can't leave your own politics at the door when you enter the museum [as a museum or archive professional], but you have to be transparent and open about those".

For Antrobus, the ideal of institutional activism remains an unsettled proposition, as she emphasises the need to hold space for informed debate and contention on divisive issues in the public sphere. However, Antrobus also recognised the role of the institution in advancing what we are terming in this book a *protest memory ethos*. This refers to how cultural institutions lend their authority and resources to furthering visibility and legitimacy to social justice campaigns and struggles, and to use protest pasts as a 'way in' to such work. As Antrobus notes, "it's not just about saving this sort of thing [the material culture and residues of protest], it's about encouraging people to go and do this sort of thing"—that is, to protest. Such discussions highlight the nuanced, sensitive and multi-directional ways in which institutions and their staff approach issues of contention, debate and civic and professional responsibility. Within this, 'memory' can be seen as a connective thread bringing such concerns and approaches together. A protest memory ethos is not just about preserving protest artefacts in collecting institutions; it's about bringing people, their emotions and their stories further into collections and the work of organisations, to make such concerns and bodies 'live', accessible and relevant. It brings into view how informed connections between past, present and future can support socially engaged practice. This ethos underscores how cultural institutions and individual heritage workers can mobilise activist memory materials to create new critical imaginaries, even solidarities, to make newly just worlds thinkable and actionable.

NOTES

1. See Chidgey (2020) for the origin story of the Women's March. Early on women of colour critiqued the Women's March for being appropriative of Black protest memory and for not being inter-sectional in practice (the original name of the march was Million Women March, a remediation of a 1997 march to empower Black communities). Consequently, coalitional work was undertaken to ensure greater racial diversity in the state chapter and national leadership committees (Moss and Maddrell 2017; Mackie and Crozier-De Rosa 2022). In later years, the national leadership was critiqued for supporting anti-Semitism. For an online documen-tation of the Women's March and how it evolved from a protest march to a political movement, see https://www.womensmarch.com.

2. White women were a significant voting bloc for Trump, further composed by socio-economic class. A 2016 post-election survey of voters indicated that 47% of white women voted for Trump in comparison to 45% for Clinton. This contrasted to 98% of Black women and 67% of Hispanic women who cast their vote for Clinton (Pew Research Center 2018).

3. Adopted as an activist policy, these eight principles of unity were shaped by activist leaders from various movements. They encompassed ending sexual violence and securing reproductive rights, LGBTQI+ rights, workers' rights, civil rights, disability rights, immigrant rights and environmental justice, making the Women's March more than just a straightforward anti-Trump march.

4. See www.facebook.com/wmwarchivesproject. The Women's March digital repository of oral histories, photographs, mixed materials and video is available at https://ufdc.ufl.edu/collections/womens march.

5. Contemporary collecting is not new but is being formalised in recent years. For a discussion of how curators at the Smithsonian National Museum of American History collected from African American and American Indian civil rights struggles and reform movements in the 1960s and 1970s, see Kylie Message (2014), *Museums and Social Activism: Engaged Protest*. There are some parallels but also points of departure with this chapter's case studies, as Message notes: "The arbitrary nature of collecting material culture from contemporary protest and reform movements throughout the 1960s and 1970s was reflected by the Smithsonian's equally ad hoc approach to archiving information and documentation about the events and curatorial contributions from this period. This situation partly arose because curators were often collecting informally, without the guidance of a collections development policy, and often also without the approval of the museum" (Message 2014, p. 20).

6. Research interviews were conducted by Red Chidgey at the sites of the case study organisations. The research participants were: Nicky Hilton, then Digital Archives Manager at Bishopsgate Institute (interviewed 26 July 2017); Adam Jaffer, then Collections Officer, and Helen Antrobus, then Programme and Events Officer, at the People's History Museum (interviewed 31 July 2017); Corinna Gardner, then Acting Keeper of the Design, Architecture and Digital department at the V&A (interviewed 23 August 2017).

7. The online news database LexisNexis was consulted using the keywords 'Women's March', 'museum', 'archive'. A search of English-language publications and newswires between the dates 12 January and 12 July 2017 returned a dataset of forty-four relevant entries. This was supplemented by a Google search of the same

keywords, to access art and business publications reporting on the march, the Pussyhat and collecting initiatives.

8. Hilton was ambiguous about the mainstream media attention the Pussyhat acquired, in part because the hats did not convey specific messages or political demands. She noted, "[I] suppose maybe that's an easier message to understand, even though it's a very vague one".

9. Hilton observed that many donors maintained their copyright, which was unusual. Typically, donors sign copyright over to the archive to ensure the material is made as accessible as possible: "They usually remove that barrier because they don't want to keep being contacted all the time". There may be several reasons for this: the contemporary nature of the event and the 'liveness' of the protest memory; the increased literacy about intellectual property in the social media age; or even that this copyright option was the first box on the form, which may have been filled out quickly. On a related note, Jayna Zweiman applied for a trademark of "Pussyhat" in 2017, as the inventor of the term and the movement. This demonstrates the increased attention to issues of copyright, intellectual property and cultural labour in activist networks, especially as activist movements can be prone to commercial exploitation. For a discussion of the relation between copyright, activism and cultural memory, see Chidgey (2018).

10. Jo Robinson was interviewed for the *Sisterhood and After* oral history project (2010–2011) at the British Library. A video clip of her discussing the Miss World (1970) protest is available at https://www.bl.uk/collection-items/jo-robinson-miss-world-contest. As an example of *memory in activism*, Robinson's Women's March placard is a remediation of the AIDS activist slogan 'Don't Mourn, Organize!'. In turn, this slogan remediates a statement from executed US labour activist Joe Hill (1879–1915).

11. Intersectionality emerges from Black feminist thought and examines how systems of inequity based on gender, race, ethnicity, class, sexual orientation, disability and other forms of oppression intersect (see Crenshaw 2017). The sign "Middle Class and PROUD!" appears to disarticulate intersectional thinking as it visibly and discursively recentres privilege. The specifics of this sign can be put into conversation with a *Vox* article reporting on the Women's March in the US (Desmond-Harris 2017). With

a close echo of terms, Desmond-Harris' article notes that white and class-privileged activists are increasingly being "asked to check their privilege", especially in enflamed Twitter arguments online. The author suggests that while many activists see this request as "unfair and aggravating", this intervention offers a chance to reflect on what an intersectional politics could be, and how a coalitional politics might emerge, rather than a retrenchment of structural advantage.

12. Carney demonstrates how the discourse #AllLivesMatter claims a "universality that is inclusive of all", but instead works "to collapse the specificities of different groups' experiences in favour of a color-blind ideology that favors white supremacy" (2016, p. 194). The extension of 'All Lives Matter'—which is not a neutral or innocent discourse—to animals enacts a similar mechanism of erasure and undermines the significance and urgency of Black Lives Matter as a racial justice movement.

13. The PHM has an object file for every acquisition which contains correspondence and context around donations (Jaffer notes that most artefacts in the permanent collection as a whole do not have such documentation in place). When a donor shares personal stories, this is included in the object file which is made accessible to researchers on-site. The system is paper-based, and emails must be printed. Jaffer notes: "In an ideal world, museums are starting to document electronically these personal narratives of things", which Hilton was exploring, as noted in the discussion above of the BI.

14. Orphan works are creative works for which the rights holder is unknown or cannot be found. Researchers have demonstrated how orphan works make up a significant portion of the material collections of GLAM institutions in the UK and beyond, and that orphan work licensing schemes in the UK remain restrictive in scope and practice (Martinez and Terras 2019). Notably a full run of *Spare Rib* (1972–1993), the leading UK women's liberation magazine, digitised by the British Library, was closed in 2020 following the UK's departure from the European Union (EU). In its creation, the digitised magazine relied heavily on EU orphan works directive. This directive allows in-copyright material held by cultural institutions to be made available where rights holders cannot, after due diligence searches, be identified (https://blogs.bl.uk/socialsci ence/2019/10/spare-rib-update.html).

15. The Pussyhat pattern design was produced by Kat Coyle, owner of the Los Angeles-based Little Knittery store. The illustrations to the visual manifesto and knitting pattern were created by Aurora Lady.

16. For a discussion of the exclusionary aspects of the Pussyhat and the Women's March, see Gökarıksel and Smith (2017). The Pussyhat Project issued a blog post on 14 January 2018 in the run-up to the second edition of the march, asking for further suggestions about what the project should do next: "Some feel that the pink color of the hat excludes people of color from the project. Some feel that the hat is a literal symbol of female anatomy, promoting Trans-Exclusionary Radical Feminism (TERF). Thank you for speaking up with your criticisms. We hear you". The post attracted 59 comments. One poster reflected: "I suggest we choose a new hat style and pattern for 2018! Let the pink pussy hats become an artifact of history—an artifact of good intentions, of community conversation, and learning. Let them stand for women of historic privilege LISTENING and MAKING CHANGES out of respect for those members of our community with the least societal privilege. Jayna, I suggest that you open up a process for knit artists to propose new hat designs that are more inclusive, and have a diverse committee (with black, brown, and trans women strongly represented) select and promote something new for the next women's marches. I wouldn't do a community vote. That is just inviting more division" (https://www.pussyhatproject.com/blog/2018/1/14/the-project-of-pussyhat).

17. The V&A is a world-recognised museum dedicated to art and design, with colonial roots dating back to 1852. It operates as a non-departmental public body of the Department for Digital, Culture, Media and Sport and is the largest institution in our study.

18. Gardner notes conservation issues with Rapid Response materials as "objects are inexpensive, so the colours, the dyes, the inks are more fugitive". Items routinely come off display and are replaced by others from the collection due to light sensitivity.

19. See https://www.pussyhatproject.com/faq. The Design Museum, London, shortlisted the Pussyhat in its Fashion Design of the Year category in 2017. The V&A reported high volumes of requests for the Pussyhat to go on loan. Consequently, it coordinated with the

Pussyhat Project in 2019 to seek further donations (https://www.pussyhatproject.com/blog/2019/9/17/want-your-pussyhat-in-a-museum).

20. Malcom et al (2020) conducted a qualitative study with 71 Pussyhat 'maker-wearers', from a survey of 511 participants of the 2017 Women's March in the US. The maker-wearers were aged between 26 and 76 years old, overwhelmingly white (78%), highly educated (89% held at least a bachelor's degree with 58% holding a graduate degree) and heterosexual (93%). Many of these participants used the words 'unity' and 'solidarity' to describe the symbolism of the pink Pussyhat. In contrast, 12 out of 219 non-Pussyhat-wearers noted the Pussyhats served as a symbol marginalising women of colour and/or people who are trans*, with the hats "primarily worn by White women" and created to "make cis gender women feel connected". With regard to the relatively low numbers who critiqued, the researchers observe that the survey was conducted shortly after the protest event, when "little dissent regarding the Pussyhat was expressed through the mainstream media" (2020, p. 13).

21. On the use of the curators' social media accounts to solicit materials, Gardner reflected: "We could have asked the museum to do it [...] It's interesting, because that's where the narrative or the personal choices of the curator impinge or impact on how the process of acquisition has happened".

22. Two further Pussyhats were accessioned in 2020 (maker: Courtney Case). See: https://collections.vam.ac.uk/item/O15 34105/pussy-hat-knitted-hat-courtney-case. Notably, in 2021, the V&A developed digital strategies to unite object, library and archive data with editorial content on its website. The 'You May Also Like' feature generates hyperlinks to other collection items, through digitised visual images. This enables users to discover objects serendipitously and, as a by-product, enables new (digital) protest memories to be made. From the Collections page for "Pussy Hat", users are directed to the *Fierce Pussy* zine (c. 1991–1996, US) and a Pussy Riot poster (designed 2012, printed 2018, Russia).

23. Object details and the Rapid Response gallery text for the Pussyhat can be accessed here: https://collections.vam.ac.uk/item/O13 80522/pussy-power-hat-zweiman-jayna.

24. See https://www.pussyhatproject.com/blog/2017/2/17/the-sea-of-pink.
25. International Women's Day (IWD) emerged from labour movements at the turn of the twentieth century in North America and across Europe. The date (8 March) is strongly linked to the 1917 women's movements of the Russian Revolution. IWD was officially recognised by the United Nations in 1977.
26. #DayWithoutAWoman was a strike action held on 8 March 2017, coordinated by the Women's March and the International Women's Strike movement to draw attention to women's contribution to society and their unpaid labour. Women were encouraged to refrain from working or consuming, and to wear red as a sign of solidarity.
27. The PHM collects across the party-political spectrum. However, Jaffer notes the difficulties associated with developing collections around contemporary populism and reactionary movements. Firstly, with collecting from the far right-wing (including "staff safety" in attending rallies; right-wing participants being "very suspicious" of mainstream collecting institutions). Secondly, "if you start collecting stuff that's very, very right wing, you alienate your existing audience".
28. On the fifth anniversary of the inaugural Women's March, the PHM featured a blog post where local resident, Caroline Dyer, recalls her experience of creating the placard "From the City of Pankhurst With Love" (Manchester being the birthplace of suffragette leader Emmeline Pankhurst, 1858–1928). As Dyer (2022) relates, her experience of the Women's March inspired her to start a new feminist organisation *Heard Storytelling*, which mobilises personal stories to create social change. In addition, Dyer turned her Women's March placard into a print to raise money for women's charities protecting the safety of sex workers and domestic violence survivors. These trajectories demonstrate the materialities and 'feminist afterlives' of protest (Chidgey 2018). In the blog post, Dyer narrates what it meant for her to see her (ephemeral) protest sign included in the PHM's permanent collection, and the importance of seeing this sign put into conversation with historically significant protest artefacts: "Towards the end of the march, I gave my banner to someone walking next to me and forgot about it. 14 months later I was booking an event at the People's History

Museum and I couldn't believe what I saw … my placard was the main picture advertising the event. I learnt it was to be displayed next to an original Suffragette banner, in an exhibition celebrating the centenary of the first women achieving the right to vote. It was one of the few moments where I really realised that my opinions matter and that I count".

29. The PHM exhibition *Represent! Voices 100 Years On* (2 June 2018 to 3 February 2019) took curatorial inspiration from feminist zines. It crowd-sourced submissions of artefacts and testimonies from citizens and activists on the theme of representation and put them into conversation with items from the permanent collection (https://phm.org.uk/exhibitions/represent-voices-100-years-on).

REFERENCES

BBC. 2017. 'Pussyhat' Knitters Join Long Tradition of Crafty Activism, January 19. Available: https://www.bbc.co.uk/news/world-us-canada-386 66373. Accessed 9 Oct 2022.

Black, S. 2017. KNIT + RESIST: Placing the Pussyhat Project in the Context of Craft Activism. *Gender, Place & Culture* 24 (5): 696–710.

Carney, N. 2016. All Lives Matter, but So Does Race: Black Lives Matter and the Evolving Role of Social Media. *Humanity & Society* 40 (2): 180–199.

Cascone, S. 2017. The Pussyhat, Beloved Icon of Women's March, Enters the V&A's Permanent Collection. *ArtNet*, March 8. Available: https://news.art net.com/art-world/victoria-and-albert-museum-pussy-hat-884771. Accessed 9 Oct 2022.

Chidgey, R. 2018. *Feminist Afterlives. Assemblage Memory in Activist Times.* Cham: Palgrave Macmillan.

Chidgey, R. 2020. How to Curate a 'Living Archive': The Restlessness of Activist Time and Labour. In *Social Movements, Cultural Memory and Digital Media: Mobilising Mediated Remembrance*, ed. S. Merrill, E. Keightley, and P. Daphi, 225–248. Cham: Palgrave Macmillan.

Crenshaw, K. 2017. *On Intersectionality: Essential Writings.* New York: The New Press.

Debono, S. 2021. Collecting Pandemic Phenomena: Reflections on Rapid Response Collecting and the Art Museum. *Collections: A Journal for Museum and Archives Professionals* 17 (2): 179–185.

Desmond-Harris, J. 2017. To Understand the Women's March on Washington, You Need to Understand Intersectional Feminism. It's Much Bigger Than "Check Your Privilege". *Vox*, January 21. Available: https://www.vox.com/identities/2017/1/17/14267766/womens-march-on-washington inauguration-trump-feminism-intersectionaltiy-race-class. Accessed 9 Oct 2022.

Dyer, C. 2022. From a March to a Museum. Revisiting the 2017 Women's Marches. People's History Museum, January 21. Available: https://phm.org.uk/blogposts/from-a-march-to-a-museum. Accessed 9 Oct 2022.

Gökarıksel, B., and S. Smith. 2017. Intersectional Feminism Beyond U.S. Flag Hijab and Pussy Hats in Trump's America. *Gender, Place & Culture* 24 (5): 628–644.

Heaney, M. 2018. Making Protest Great Again. *Contexts* 17: 1. Available: https://journals.sagepub.com/doi/full/10.1177/1536504218766550. Accessed 9 Oct 2022.

Janes, R.R., and R. Sandell, eds. 2019. *Museum Activism*. London: Routledge.

Lee-Crossett, K. 2018. *Collecting Change/Changing Collections*. Available: https://heritage-futures.org/collecting-changechanging-collections-report-goals-challenges-contemporary-collecting. Accessed 9 Oct 2022.

Mackie, V., and S. Crozier-De Rosa. 2022. Rallying Women: Activism, Archives and Affect. *Women's History Review* 31 (6): 975–1001.

Malcom, N.L., A.K. Martindale, V.A. Paulins, J.L. Hillery, and A. Howell. 2020. Unifying Yet Dividing: Voices of Pussyhat Maker–Wearers Who Participated in the 2017 Women's Marches. *Fashion and Textiles* 7: 32. Available: https://link.springer.com/article/10.1186/s40691-020-00218-5.

Marshall, A. 2018. Posters, Banners, Boarding Passes: Museums Try to Get a Head Start on History. *The New York Times*, June 18. Available: https://www.nytimes.com/2018/06/18/arts/design/rapid-response-collecting-ireland-berlin.html. Accessed 20 Apr 2023.

Martinez, M., and M. Terras. 2019. 'Not Adopted': The UK Orphan Works Licensing Scheme and How the Crisis of Copyright in the Cultural Heritage Sector Restricts Access to Digital Content. *Open Library of Humanities* 5 (1): 1–51.

McIntyre, L. 2018. *Post-Truth*. Cambridge: MIT Press.

Message, K. 2014. *Museums and Social Activism: Engaged Protest*. New York: Routledge.

Moss, P., and A. Maddrell. 2017. Emergent and Divergent Spaces in the Women's March: The Challenges of Intersectionality and Inclusion. *Gender, Place & Culture* 24 (5): 613–620.

Pew Research Center. 2018. For Most Trump Voters, 'Very Warm' Feelings for Him Endured. Available: https://www.pewresearch.org/politics/2018/08/09/an-examination-of-the-2016-electorate-based-on-validated-voters. Accessed 9 Oct 2022.

Salahu-Din, D.T. 2019. Documenting the Black Lives Matter Movement in Baltimore through Contemporary Collecting: An Initiative of the National Museum of African American History and Culture. *Collections: A Journal for Museum and Archive Professionals* 15 (2–3): 101–112.

CHAPTER 5

Activist Memory and the Archive

Abstract This chapter provides case study two on the archive as catalyst for remembering; in this case, climate protest and the forgetting of urban water. Drawing upon the work of the arts activism group Platform who since 1983 have campaigned on climate-related issues, the chapter covers one strand of their activism focused on London's rivers, polluted water and provocations for the regeneration of the city's watershed. The chapter analyses two museum re-exhibitions of Platform's *Still Waters* (1992) campaign, and Platform's sustained reflections on the campaign and the acquisition of Platform's collection into an archive. A key consideration in this remembering and archiving of Platform's activism is the inclusion of informal, lay or activist memories that serve as grassroots intermediaries and paratexts. The connectivity of this process of archiving climate protest with official media archives (television, film and journalism) and the socially mediated memories of protesting river neglect has significance internationally with other urban river daylighting campaigns.

Keywords Environmental activism · Archive · Sustainability · Rivers · London · Daylighting

R. Chidgey and J. Garde-Hansen, *Museums, Archives and Protest Memory*, Palgrave Macmillan Memory Studies, https://doi.org/10.1007/978-3-031-44478-4_5

Introduction: 'Waters of Forgetfulness'

In 1985, Ivan Illich published *H₂O and the Waters of Forgetfulness* which explored the materialisation of water as other things—H₂O, man-made lakes, indoor plumbing, a cleaning fluid and much more. The book is a lament on the increasing scientific technocracy and control surrounding water, as it turns into something else, becoming a memory of itself. Such a mediated social construction of water as memory has been recently explored by one of the authors of this book in *Media and Water: Communication, Culture and Perception* (Garde-Hansen 2021). The chemical formula of water (H_2O), said Illich, "is a social creation of modern times, a resource that is scarce and that calls for technical management. It is an observed fluid that has lost the ability to mirror the water of dreams. The city child has no opportunities to come in touch with living water" (Illich 1985, p. 76). Reclaiming water was for Illich to remember, recover and unearth the mystical, cultural and social relations that had been forgotten. When interviewed for this chapter, it was Illich's book that is pointed to as the inspiration for the arts activist group Platform (1983–present) to produce their campaign *Still Waters* in London in 1992. The process of remembering this activist campaign over the last 30 years by the Museum of the River Thames, the Museum of London, media outlets, the activist group itself and the Bishopsgate Institute speaks to the afterlives of protest and the protest memory framework we have been exploring in this book.

Thus far, we have addressed debates within the museum, archive and heritage sector around protest, and we have explored museums and archives with histories of collecting protest materials and institutional-led engagements with activism. Recently, museums have stepped up to make a statement on their support of climate activism (ICOM 2022). For many decades the activities of environmental activists in and around cultural spaces and their use of culture and art within *urban spaces of neglect* were largely ignored by museums and archives as activities to be collected, remembered and stored. No longer can museums and archives afford to forget histories of climate activism, thus drawing upon the media-memory-activism nexus to connect the public with lesser-known environmental histories. In this final case study, we are moving away from Connerton's (2008, p. 65) 'Seven Types of Forgetting' wherein to "say that something has been stored—in an archive, in a computer—is tantamount to saying that, though it is in principle always retrievable, we can afford to forget it". Instead, we discovered Platform's work affording a 'living archive' of activist knowledge that is always resurfacing through the media-memory-activism nexus connected by museums, galleries, exhibition spaces, mainstream and social media, and archives as a slowly unfolding ecology of protest memory.

The burden of memory, or the desire for all memory to be wiped, may be an extinction-level fantasy for those troubled by pasts, yet for Connerton, he notes that the natural sciences feel an acute need to discard, that every scientist learns how to forget, in order not to be "crippled by chronic over-information" (2008, p. 66). What is missing from this characterisation of forgetting is the growing demand that museums and archives remember the histories of the natural world's entanglements with human stories. Engagement with the GLAM sector, particularly by publicly engaged scientists as well as climate activists, seeks to connect the public to sustainable memories of protest, risk, resilience and environmental citizenship (see Garde-Hansen et al. 2016). In fact, while the 'imperial archives' such as the Royal Geographical Society, the British Museum, the Royal Society may all be contributing to a "cultural surfeit of information" (Connerton 2008, p. 65), they have also begun reconnecting communities to memories of plants, animals, species, extreme weather, climate change and how past human communities have and have not adapted to risk. They are becoming reimagined as *climate witnesses* and along with environmental activists and community action groups are beginning to be more than active bystanders in environmental violence (or as Nixon [2011] states "slow violence").[1]

While we have been exploring in this book the liveness of protest for museums and archives, there is also a liveness to archiving protest itself as activists seek remembrance and memorability from trusted cultural organisations. One of the key issues we considered when researching the importance of contemporary social justice and environmental struggles was to recognise that protest memory re-surfaces in the current socially mediated ecosystem, exposing deeper roots of engagement with archives and museums through different media forms and over a longer period of time. This means the media-memory-activism nexus is composed of a cultural archaeology of a variety of creative, media and artistic formats and forms, crafted and re-crafted through digitally connective media. In this chapter we address Nixon's and Illich's fears that forgetfulness is systematically and structurally built in to how communities move on from and 'recover' from the loss of their environment as their memories are displaced:

> Attritional catastrophes that overspill clear boundaries in time and space are marked above all by displacements – temporal, geographical, rhetorical, and technological displacements that simplify violence and underestimate, in advance and in retrospect, the human and environmental costs. Such displacements smooth the way to amnesia, as places are rendered irretrievable to those who once inhabited them, places that ordinarily pass unmourned in the corporate media. (Nixon 2011, p. 7)

For Londoners (like many inhabitants of cities built on watersheds and basins) citizens have forgotten that streams and rivers flow beneath them, captured by the nineteenth-century engineering and technological solution of canalisation only coming into view as the climate changes and extreme weather events increase pluvial and fluvial flooding. Yet, arts activist collectives such as Platform have been drawing together political and aesthetic objectives, building actions, campaigns and interventions around imagining London differently and reminding the public of forgotten environments since the early 1990s. In her recent book *Creating Worlds Otherwise: Art, Collective Action, and (Post) Extractivism* (2022), Paula Serafini focuses on the social role of arts activists and organisations drawing on examples from Argentina and the UK, developing a paradigm around autonomous movements, rights of nature, environmental justice and transition discourses. For Serafini arts activism is oriented towards 'worlding', in which new narratives for living and alternative visions for the future are foregrounded, drawing upon her own collaborations with Platform. This chimes with Boaventura de Sousa Santos' *Epistemologies of the South* (2014), which considers who has been excluded from defining the problems never mind finding the solutions to environmental and global social justice:

> The answer that Western thought gives to this question is weak because it only recognises the problems that can be discussed within the Cartesian epistemological and ontological model. [...] global capitalism has never been so avid for natural resources as today, to the extent that it is legitimate to speak of a new extractivist imperialism. Land, water, and minerals have never been so coveted, and the struggle for them has never had such disastrous social and environmental consequences. (de Sousa Santos 2014, p. 23)

Similarly, 'to world' and remember London's rivers differently and to demand their unburying[2] is defined in the interviews with Jane Trowell,[3] former Arts Educator for Platform, as a protest against the imperialist agenda towards the natural world, as she recalls the group's intentions in 1992:

> We had a very ideological position. The mistake of waterborne sewage as a techno fix, as a Victorian technofix. The disaster of waterborne sewage. Which was always hailed as a great example of Victorian engineering...of British greatness. So there was a kind of imperial angle... a critique of.... supremacist techno fixes that we then exported everywhere. The flushed toilet being a bit of a disaster. An activist agenda to tangibly say, these need to be dug up, that this was a mistake. We were very much against a kind of historicising, pastoral or nostalgia. We were very much in the line of 'this was a mistake'. This river, this entire watershed, needs to be reconceived as an ecosystem.

Through interviews with Trowell we have drawn out her multiple and overlapping roles as artist, educator, researcher, unofficial memory archivist, as well as activist donor and curator, exhibitor, blogger and campaigner on this need to remember London's rivers (among many other issues about which she has been active). Through a multiplicity of roles and cultural work over a long career, traversing the analogue to digital mediascapes, Trowell and her colleagues[4] were committed to securing the protest memory of Platform's early work in the 1980s and they have meaningfully engaged with official memory institutions, archivists, researchers and students. In this chapter we explore Trowell's ethos of protest memory preservation and activation and how this aligns with the existing objectives of the museum and archival activism of the Bishopsgate Institute and other cultural organisations. The spotlight here is not on institutional-led contemporary collecting, curation and archival information management. The chapter focuses on the activist donor's experiences of collecting, managing and negotiating the preservation of material that documents a slow developing, often invisible, climate emergency struggle in the heart of London at a time when there was much less cultural and arts engagement with British waterways, rivers and coasts than there is today.

STILL WATERS (1992)

Platform (https://platformlondon.org) is an arts activism organisation founded in 1983 and while often focused on the impacts of the global oil industry, London's lost rivers was one of several issues the artists addressed in the early years. Based in London, the group has evolved over time to address social and ecological injustices in the city as well as covering anti-nuclear protest, anti-racism, workers' rights and student protests, always with an arts and education approach. Street theatre, music, agitprop, installations, exhibitions, writing, sound art, video, social sculpture and performance are combined with educational outreach and materials, school visits and festivals and training workshops. The projects during the early 1990s on London's rivers were particularly influential and foreshadow the recent debates around water quality, flooding, making room for rivers, and pollution. Even Boris Johnson, as Mayor of London, popularised resurfacing London's lost rivers in his 2008–2009 support for the London Rivers Action Plan (2009) that sought to resurface 15 km of London's rivers by 2015, a target led by the Environment Agency and was exceeded. While *daylighting* urban rivers has become a sustainable urban drainage solution in recent years in several cities,[5] Platform were significantly ahead of the game, placing imagination in opposition to science and story-ing water in ways that promoted unearthing the past. As Amitav Ghosh (2016, p. 9) has pointed out, the "climate crisis is also a crisis of culture, and thus of the imagination" and to create desire for London's rivers was to imagine the city differently.

In May 1992 Platform delivered a month-long programme of arts interventions and activities to explore the 'unburying' of four London rivers: the Fleet, Walbrook, Effra and Wandle.[6] At the time of researching for the *Afterlives of Protest Research Network* in 2018–2019, the place the public could learn about these past activist projects was Platform's website which provided a repository of project materials from the 1980s and 1990s. Jane Trowell passed along to the authors the original project description at this now defunct hyperlink 'https://platformlondon.org/otherprojects.asp#stillwater'. It was from this link that the researchers learned the details of the project while collaborating with Trowell in the *Afterlives of Protest Research Network*. However, the person responsible for IT security at Platform discovered in the early 2020s that the 'old website' of project materials and descriptions being 'housed' in the new website data architecture were a security risk and so these pages disappeared during the writing of this chapter. *Moved but not gone*, memories of the webpage can be found (in skeletal form and without images) in the Internet Archive's Wayback Machine (IAWM), re-born as a ghost of the *Still Waters* project.[7] These original project descriptions now also require unburying and the IAWM page is important for recording the diversity and breadth of the sub-projects that combined to produce *Still Waters*.

Still Waters consisted of several interventions. *Listening to the Fleet* (which involved interviewing, performance, dowsing, clay-inscription on London clay tablets and fired along the riverbank) ensured passers-by became enthused as they discussed unburying the Fleet. *The Power of the Wandle* sought to reinstate the Wandle's 9000-year history by commissioning a sculptor and an economist to re-shape the public's appreciation of the river through public meetings, walks and a night-time performance. *Swimming in the Walbrook* (social actions, events, rituals and performance) sought to mark a neglected river's movement beneath the city and the financial quarter. It brought together a psychologist and artist to explore more deeply the reality of a great river confined to a storm drain and disconnected from the humans above. *Unearthing the Effra* employed marketing and advertising strategies (with artist and publicist working with the community) to establish a performative campaign through a very convincing pop-up 'Effra Redevelopment Agency' (Fig. 5.1).

As the IAWM page describing the *Unearthing of the Effra* states:

> Dreams become real when spoken, and to hear the word Effra on hundreds of people's lips, on radio programmes, to see it on billboards and in newspapers began the journey along the road to the Effra's revival. The Effra project was deliberately constructed to be a highly convincing simulacra of a Docklands 'development agency' aesthetic, and some would say too convincing for its own ethical good, and continues to raise hackles and chuckles when we present it today.[8]

The four projects were interlinked and developed together. Not only did they have an afterlife as they were remembered by communities and Platform developed them into future projects,[9] but they became protest memory in numerous remediated ways (anniversaries,[10] new exhibitions, salvaging of materials, media interviews). Trowell herself actively remembered them (in the many talks and presentations over the years) before

Fig. 5.1 'Effra Redevelopment Agency' poster of the 'imagined ERA' that was presented as a real proposition (Platform, May 1992). Photograph Jane Trowell, 2019

being archived at the Bishopsgate Institute, a process that began in 2016. It is this movement of protest memory and the liveness of archiving memories of *Still Waters* that the rest of this chapter will explore in interconnected and overlapping techniques that speak to a protest memory method and ethos. These techniques of *re-exhibition* by two different museums at different points in time speak to the dynamic of museums emerging as *co-creators of protest memory*, as the re-exhibition of activist materials were integrated with exhibits from the museums' own collections, saw wider community-based collaborations and developed a series of public programmes and outputs. This involved stitching together the work of the two museum exhibitions, with the activists' memory work, and through talks, workshops, educational materials and media interviews. The official archival acquisition of Platform's collection by the Bishopsgate Institute, we shall show below, reveals the dynamic of *protector and carer* of protest memory, which becomes an activist-archivist technique in itself.

THE 'MUSEUM OF...': CO-CREATION OF CLIMATE PROTEST MEMORY

It takes some unburying of the web to find evidence of the 'Museum Of ...' series (five temporary museums from 1998 to 2001 curated by Clare Patey and Pippa Bailey).[11] We can locate evidence online of the pop-up museum installations through broken links, pages moved and half-sentence traces on Google search results to be cut and pasted back into Google to locate where those summary texts might be replicated. Trowell had also struggled to find evidence online of Platforms' *Water, Land, Fire* (2001) physical installation (about the Fleet) that had spun off from the *Still Waters* (1992) project and became part of the fifth and final 'Museum Of the River Thames' (March–July 2001) staged at the Bargehouse, London. As a temporary pop-up 'museum' promoted through supplementary but fairly rudimentary webpages of text, images and video, we need the activist memories of Trowell to better understand the one screen capture of the 'Museum Of the River Thames' we found on IAWM from 10 July 2001. The London Metropolitan Archives (LMA), where the Museum Of... collection is now held, describes the project of the Museum of the River Thames as "telling a story" of the "environment and personal relationship with the river", covering found objects, drawings and installations, noting it as a collaboration with the London Rivers Authority, the Thames Explorer Trust, the Millennium Bridge Trust, Platform and the Museum of London.[12]

However, the IAWM screen capture notes the museum was sponsored by Thames Water and the water company state at the bottom of the screen capture: "In collaboration with The Museum Of we have jointly created a rare opportunity for people of all backgrounds and ages to explore their relationship with the river and contribute their own experience of the Thames to this innovative exhibition".[13] Thames Water, in its early days of German ownership, could have used the exhibition for good public relations, but it was indeed 'rare' and innovative for a water company to engage with artist-activists in this way. Trowell recalls the commissioning of artists to paint the floor of the Bargehouse (gold lettering by Miche Fabre Lewin and a watershed floor map by Tod Hanson) with the Thames watershed (Thames Valley) in gold on blue, suspending a boat in the space and running three 5-hour walks along the course of the River Fleet from Hampstead to Blackfriars, which was "packed with walkers—thirty each time".

The temporary nature of the Museum of the River Thames lasting only five months in 2001, speaks to the precarity of the museum itself as a participatory agent and site of protest memory as well as water memory, particularly when curators are experimenting with culture, place, identity and the future of the museum. Pop-up museums would become more common from the 2010s onwards as traditional museums sought to engage the public, where the public were, or create new audiences and conversations around objects brought to unusual places. Nevertheless, evidence of Thames Water's sponsorship captured by the IAWM also indicates the early role of a private water company as creator of water's cultural memories in the city. A role that has continued in the English privatised system as public relations and heritage-making from the main water companies. Thames Water today is the custodian of the very 'imperial' and 'technofix' heritage solutionism that *Still Waters* critiqued in the early 1990s while persistently being fined millions of pounds for polluting rivers with sewage in eleven cases over the last decade.[14] Hiding commercial and public utility failure behind 'heritage days out' is a kind of culture-washing that is concerned with the extraction of value from water and its past engineering, not the imagining of a new social contract with the public and new technological solutions to climate change.

Thus, the 'Museum of the River Thames' (and the whole series) is remembered by Trowell as "quite exceptional", a "museological experiment", "quite extraordinary" and a "complete triumph" of participatory arts and activism, with the Museum of London lending Samuel Scott's painting *Entrance to the Fleet River, London* c1793 to be displayed. Yet, she also states for the "Museum Of...", unfortunately, the project was not archived". Therefore, Trowell shares a photo from her collection of the installation (Fig. 5.2) to give a sense of what visitors experienced.

It is the important protest memory dynamic of archiving the museum's techniques as an agent and site of climate activism that is so vital to

Fig. 5.2 A low resolution snapshot from Jane Trowell of *Water, Land, Fire* (2001)

the protest memory ethos we have explored in this book. If not remembered and archived, then future water-stressed publics will have to start again and will not have the specific local water memory resources for challenging state and utility providers on their failures. Moreover, the role of the IAWM in capturing earlier webpages of such temporary museum projects reveals a great deal about the politics of water and representation that artists and museums have to negotiate.

THE MUSEUM OF LONDON AS CO-CREATOR (BUT NOT CARER) OF CLIMATE PROTEST MEMORY

A well-archived museum project was the *Secret Rivers* exhibition curated by Tom Ardill and Kate Sumnall at the Museum of London (MoL) which ran 24 May–27 October 2019. This featured a re-exhibition of the Effra Watershed model that had been part of 'Unearthing the Effra' from *Still Waters* 1992. Platform was invited to contribute through re-exhibition and funding was provided by the MoL to re-stage the model which by then had fallen into disrepair: as with many arts and activism projects, installations and materials are stored in less-than-ideal conditions. The Effra Redevelopment Agency, part of *Still Waters*, had been devised by artist John (now Jay) Jordan and curator Andrea Philips. The original watershed model had been designed by Katie Lloyd-Thomas in 1992 and Platform commissioned architect Sahra Hersi to restore and reinvent the Effra Watershed model (Fig. 5.3) for the new display. This allowed the MoL to draw into its existing collections a history of activism and thus operate as a domain of protest memory through a reinstallation of the restored model in collaboration with the activists, and co-creator of protest memory as parts of *Still Waters* re-emerged and were renewed for new visitors.

The MoL's website (as of writing) still has the press release for *Secret Rivers* (2019). The *Still Waters* activist material is an important though small part of a broader desire to exhibit the MoL's collections and their connection to the hidden cultures of water in London:

Fig. 5.3 Restored and re-exhibited Effra Watershed model funded by the Museum of London, *Secret Rivers* (2019)

Secret Rivers combines art and archaeology, with mudlarking, photography, film and much more to uncover the mysteries of London's rivers, both those that flow above ground and those that have been buried beneath our feet. The exhibition shows how London has been shaped by the Thames and its tributaries, and how they have in turn been shaped by Londoners. It explores how the Effra, Fleet, Neckinger, Lea, Tyburn, Walbrook, Wandle and Westbourne have been exploited for transport and industry, enjoyed and revered, and have influenced artists and writers.[15]

Secret Rivers was well-mediated, and traces of the exhibition can be found in television news archives (e.g. *BBC London News* featured Effra with an interview with Trowell on location in Belair Park and suburban streets, 25 May 2019). In the 'daylighting' section of the exhibition the MoL commissioned a film on the digging up of the rivers which featured Jane Trowell in various spots around Brixton and beyond. A tweet from the time shows Trowell with a BBC journalist listening for the River Effra in Tulse Hill (Fig. 5.4).

Trowell was not on the team behind the idea of the 'Unearthing the Effra' project that was part of *Still Waters* (1992), but she soon became a key part of the reimagining of London as a city of rivers. The extraction and re-exhibition into *Secret Rivers* (2019) she recognises as "a visionary concept", as "getting a lot of press" at the time ("60 to 70 pieces of press, quite phenomenal") and as a "very bold project because it was aping the development agencies". All this re-investment in re-exhibiting *Still Waters* and the Effra Redevelopment Agency watershed model by the MoL in fact became re-forgotten when the MoL declined the acquisition of the model it had paid an architect to restore. The MoL had been a temporary protector and co-creator of protest memory but would not be the carer of that protest memory going forward and so Illich's "waters of forgetfulness" returned.

THE ARTIST-ACTIVIST AS PROVOCATEUR OF PROTEST MEMORY

It is clear, from our case study of museums as domains and co-creators of protest memory, that researchers must also engage with activists as collaborators and provocateurs in protest memory, particularly as analogue media materials are now held (if at all) in multiple closed or pay-walled archives or from cultural productions that are defunct or disappeared. Trowell has numerous digitised copies of newspaper articles related to *Still Waters* from the 1990s, including many from the *Unearthing the Effra*

Fig. 5.4 Tweet of BBC news journalist Michael Barrett listening for the River Effra with Jane Trowell of Platform, 21 May 2019

project as this became the most 'real' to local people and beneficiaries with numerous journalists reporting on this new ERA. The mediated memorability of the *Unearthing the Effra* also ensured it was re-exhibited in *Secret Rivers* (2019), no doubt because it had been so widely reported because the 'Effra Redevelopment Agency' performance appeared as a serious urban redevelopment project, presented to the public as real, whereas Platform knew it was a simulation, a provocation and a one-month performance.

Between 1992 and 1996 many London newspapers covered the ERA's new vision for London. For example, the article 'River Deep: A Vision' from *Croydon Leader* (28 May 1992) and 'Raise the River' in the *Kentish Times* (4 June 1992) conveyed the "mixed reaction" of the public to the scheme. "Fancy going for a sail in Brixton" in the *South London Press* (12 May 1992) not only stated that the "doubters may think such an idea will not wash" but quoted a 'Thames Water spokesman' (the very water company that would later sponsor the Museum of the River Thames 2001). He "dismissed the idea" and re-affirmed the very Victorian 'technofix' solutionism that Platform were ideologically against:

He said "About eight to nine miles of the Effra was bricked up about 100 years ago and has been used ever since as a storm relief sewer. It means whenever there is a storm, it can be used to carry excess sewerage. It is not really a practical idea, unless you want to spend millions building a new sewer. If that was to go ahead, the costs would have to be met by the public."[16]

Such a statement from the largest UK private water company is provocatively 'unearthed' by the activities of Platform in 1992 and signals how the company will go on to misuse the hidden rivers of London for the next two decades. While the *Evening Standard* will report in 'Let the Lost Rivers Flow Again' (12 February 1996) on the River Fleet that Platform has a "mad-cap idea" to dig up rivers, ultimately there is little scrutiny of Thames Water.

Trowell (and Platform) will go on to recall the lost rivers projects and remind audiences of *Still Waters* (1992) through talks and presentations. As an art historian Trowell was keenly aware that lineage, provenance and preservation really matter. Platform commissioned artist-curator Laura Plant to respond to the Platform archive and she chose to curate 'Still Waters, Still'[17] an audio and print work. There was a talk Trowell gave for Waterweek (2018) on '(De-)Sewerising London's Rivers' and a presentation to the Archives group at the Arnolfini, Bristol, 2019 on 'Archive as Catalyst' to recognise Platform's 2009 50-day exhibition there entitled *C Words: Carbon, Climate, Capital, Culture*. To staff at the Museum of London, Trowell was invited to speak by Tom Ardill in 2018, as part of their *New Conversations* in-house programme. In this talk titled 'Art-activists and the Museum' Trowell opens her presentation with the slide (Fig. 5.5) signalling the need for a protest memory ethos in UK museums

Fig. 5.5 'This is not an activist archive'. Photograph Jane Trowell

and archives. This is the storage facility of Platform's archive, in boxes, in some kind of order but uncatalogued and waiting for acquisition to Bishopsgate Institute, a process that had finally begun.

THE BISHOPSGATE INSTITUTE AS CARER AND PROTECTOR OF (MOST BUT NOT ALL) PROTEST MEMORY

There is a certain irony within Trowell's telling of the origin story of the archiving process. In 2013 Platform had loaned over 100 boxes of paper archive, audio and video, and their banner collection, 1983—c2010 to the *Special Collections and Archives on London Protest and Campaigning* at the Bishopsgate Institute (BI). That year the BI archivists began cataloguing but this was only the beginning of a longer process. Around 2016 Platform found itself having to move out of its offices by the river:

> We knew that we needed to probably move office. [. . .] We're gonna get gentrified out of our office. Which was a sort of damp, dark basement just South of Tower Bridge, very near the Thames, which we loved. [. . .] I could see the writing on the wall, that whole area. We need to empty the space. We needed to start sorting this out.

Approaching several archives and institutions and inspired by the London International Festival of Student Theatre (1981–2001) archive now held at Goldsmiths, University of London, Trowell successfully secured a research and development grant from the Arts Council England. The question all archives ask when offered such a large and eclectic collection is where are the resources for cataloguing? "Because it's not coming with any cash to catalogue, it's going to sit in boxes, it'll be safe, but it'll sit in boxes (as in Fig. 5.5) because we [the archive] can't just catalogue it". Trowell continues:

> So then somebody said to me, look at Bishopsgate Institute. They have a London collection but they also have campaigns. A special collection on campaigns. So I got in touch with the Bishopsgate Institute and I met with the lead archivist Stefan Dickers, who was COMPLETELY FABULOUS. And he embraced the whole thing [. . .] and he was absolutely thrilled that we were going to Bishopsgate for their special collection on London protesting campaigning. (*Emphasis to signal the joy the activist evokes when recalling the memory of the conversation*)

The freedom to make decisions and the energy and passion of the lead archivist at the Bishopsgate Institute seems to be a particularly important factor in Platform's decision, as well as the resources the Bishopsgate Institute found to catalogue the collection of 207 boxes, 15 oversized items and 13 rolled items.[18]

However, there are limits to an archive's ability to act within a dynamic of carer and protector of protest memory and this is an issue with the materiality of activism itself, which as we have noted in this book is not always easily preservable. Three-dimensional activist artefacts of which Platform has many, one being the restored Effra watershed model, could not go into the collection in this instance:

> They could only take paper. Paper based and flat. Panels, yes, but not anything bulky. They just don't have space [...] there are models and artworks and you know placards that they would never take. [...] And it's in the lock up, self-storage. In this light industrial estate. [...] An organised mountain of three-dimensional materials [...] And that's where the Effra watershed model is. We've really, really tried to protect it all these years [...] So that's what it is. Vulnerable. It was a vulnerable piece because it was made out of foamboard. And had little pins in it, and you can imagine it was not going to last 30 years, but now it is restored and protected.

Platform's protest memory cannot only be held in a conventional paper-based archive. It spills over (like its projects) into many dimensions and there is a new generation of Platform members and a 40-year anniversary in 2023 to consider as a moment for further memorialisation.

Conclusion: A Slow Protest Memory of Hydrocitizenship

The case of Platform as activist catalyst for remembering their own collection brings together two agents (activist and archive) who see protest memory in different modes. For the activist, their activities were and are events (interventions, exhibitions, campaigns, installations). Those events brought attention to the hidden temporalities of what forgetting polluted rivers of London has meant and still means: that the destruction of the environment had already begun, long ago but is slowly and repeatedly forgotten and will continue, if *business as usual* thinking prevails. The role played by museums and archives as (re-)catalysers (but also structures) suggest that a protest memory framework is built from the limited and contingent roles of the GLAM sector as carers and innovators in the protest memory space. In the infrastructural space of the archive, space matters of course, and there we find the mainly paper-based items from Platform—"not anything bulky" such as the watershed model, placards and artworks.[19] Here is a collection of most of the eventfulness of the activist group's actions. But in the activist's memory work (as a life story conveyed in interview), those past actions reached much further back into industrial and engineering history as much as projected a greener and cleaner future.

While the collection of activist materials is for future researchers, and records protest actions at particular points in time by engaged actors in specific places, the memory narrative of the activist reflecting on the campaign reaches even further backwards and forwards. Trowell remembers the past actions as revelations of the damage to the environment as already done and the performativity of the ERA as a believable restorative framework that captured public imagination. At the point of 'techno-solutionism' (the canalisation of London's waterways), the rupture happened: the lost connection to water, a connection to be rediscovered by arts activism over time and through campaigning. But that has to be remembered, archived and re-mediated. As Tavory and Wagner-Pacifici (2022) argue of the "radical eventfulness" of environmental activists such as Extinction Rebellion: "the climate crisis *is* happening, and *has been* happening". Thus, to remember *Still Waters* (1992) is to record the slow ongoingness of rupture and attempts at renewal.

It is evident Platform's *Still Waters* (1992) project made ripples and activated critical awareness of hidden rivers in London. Their project became memorable through the activities of museums, archives and the activists doing the memory work as much as the arts activism itself at the time. It is always difficult to measure the exact impact of a project such as *Still Waters* but it's clear in tracking the re-exhibitions, remediations and the remembering of the project that it seeded ideas, as Trowell notes:

> All sorts of books have been published, then, in the intervening 20 years. Guided walks, we did so many guided walks. You know, artists doing this project, that project, the other project. When we were researching the lost rivers of London and the buried rivers there were very, very, very few books. There was Nicholas Barton, perhaps and a few local pamphlets. So I think as an activist, I sort of think to myself. Well, you know, look, look, look at that. We were part of that. We weren't the sole reason, but we were certainly part of that boom.

That boom continues in the mainstream with a post-pandemic re-engagement of people and their neighbourhoods that has meant the daylighting of city rivers is no longer a 'mad-cap idea' but is, as reported in the *Guardian*, now a legitimate demand, such as the call to create green walking routes along London's forgotten waterways (Davies 2021). This may not be digging up London's rivers (though the de-canalisation of the River Ravensbourne at Lewisham demonstrated it is possible),[20] but it signals a slow growing hydrocitizenship through 'heritage from below'. In the case of *Still Waters* that 'below' was deep, hidden and embedded in Victorian imperialist solutions to water and sewerage.[21]

Platform's *Still Waters* (1992) is an early incarnation of an activist agenda that Garde-Hansen (2021, p. 144) has identified as a more recent "worldwide movement of river clean-ups and de-canalisation with creative, media and cultural heritage projects of public engagement". Our interviews with Trowell revealed the role that activist narratives, protest memory, creative arts practices, museums and archives play in a cultural ecosystem of counter-narratives to private industry's extractive and 'tech-nofix' solutionism. The misuse of that imperialist engineering by Thames Water for example with its pollution of the waterways is being revealed and the work to activate and make visible the hidden rivers continues. Platform's work connected to a growing *trans-national memory* approach to hidden city rivers and knowledge exchange between researchers, activists and artists that enabled communities to generate hidden river stories. This has trickled down to ordinary citizens and mainstream news accounts of privatised water companies not investing in infrastructure. To re-engage people with a cultural memory of the social life of water in cities and beyond is an activist position and works against the sustained imperial history of damming, embanking, reinventing, hiding, polluting and profiting from water.

However temporary or partial the re-exhibition of Platform's community-based and mediated storytelling projects around canalisation, de-canalisation and river cultures, they sought to create and remember good water narratives that could be recycled as urban learning in a polluted city environment. Their work resonates with a wide range of active river culture and riparian heritage projects that are seeking to change perceptions of rivers and coasts.[22] In engendering a sense of community, civic engagement and citizenship through water storyworlds, such projects tackle head on how to activate the public, how to brand and communicate water issues, the role of community in development, the loss of waterways on urban resilience and the need to archive along the way. As Lejano et al. (2013, p. 2) write:

> Stories or narratives create the glue that binds people together in networks, providing them with a sense of history, common ground, and future, thus enabling them to persist even in the context of resistance. It is through stories that people both analyse and realise personal relationships with land, animals, rivers, air, and even bacteria as well as the new technologies that impact the environment.

The memories of the lost rivers are not past and the work of protesting their loss is not over. While the violence through neglect, ignorance, complacency and weak environmental policymaking has been slowly accreting, so too have the memories of protesting the hidden waters in industrialised and engineered landscapes been slowly making their way into the wider public sphere. Nixon (2011, p. 8) states that "the past of slow violence is never past, so too the post is never fully post: indus-trial particulates and effluents live on in the environmental elements we inhabit and in our very bodies, which epidemiologically and ecologically are never our simple contemporaries". The increasing demand for places for wild swimming, for reclaiming memories of cleaner waters, all suggest that slow methods of human engagement with rivers and seas are galvanising public opinion: walking, paddleboarding, swimming, citizen monitoring, deep listening, observing and the slow and methodical work of archiving a protest that began in the 1990s is coming together. It will be met by fast and distracting public relations campaigns by water companies and socially mediated government communications.[23] While Platform's impact and activism have not been fast, accelerated, spectacular and hugely disruptive compared to more recent headline-grabbing protests, this misses the methods at work. It has been slow moving and it has been shaped by slow-moving events: gentrification (moving offices), climate change (the rivers come to the surface themselves in flash floods), decolonisation (recognising that extractivism continues) and deindustrialisation (a demand for more green city spaces). This requires the activist organisation to not only pay close and careful attention to environmental destruction, but to remember, archive and remediate and recirculate those protest memories for environmental reconstruction.

NOTES

1. Rob Nixon's concept of 'slow violence' is defined as "a violence that occurs gradually and out of sight, a violence of delayed destruction that is dispersed across time and space, an attritional violence that is typically not viewed as violence at all" (Nixon 2011, p. 2).
2. 'Unburying' is a term used by Trowell and is a synonym for what would later be termed daylighting, see note 5.
3. Jane Trowell was interviewed by Joanne Garde-Hansen on 21 December 2022. The interview data was supplemented with email correspondence on 28 April 2023 which allowed Trowell to review the interview quotations, providing further details and clarifications. All quotations referenced in this chapter refer to this date of interview and these clarifications.
4. Jane Trowell became a core member of Platform in 1991 until 2020 when she "retired after 29½ years". Her background is in art, education, art history and curating. Trowell has a political commitment to anti-racism and ecological justice issues. She came

into Platform after receiving an invitation to collaborate in the summer of 1991 on the *Still Waters* project. By December 1991 Platform had raised funds to do the work. Trowell was not a part of the group that conceived the project. At that point it was James Marriott, Dan Gretton and artist John Jordan as the core members when Platform was smaller, very activist in intention and peripatetic. Trowell became a key part of the reimagining of London as a city of rivers.

5. Wild et al. in 'Deculverting: reviewing the evidence on the "daylighting" and restoration of culverted rivers' in *Water and Environment Journal* define this as "opening up buried watercourses and restoring them to more natural conditions" (2011, p. 412). I will also use the term in this chapter metaphorically to signal the daylighting of cultural memories through opening up, rerouting and bringing to the surface media archives and cultural content that adds environmental values to communities through cultural work. See also www.daylighting.org. Platform's approach to remembering its own daylighting project is a good example of the cultural daylighting of protest memory.

6. Fleet (Hampstead & Highgate to Blackfriars), Walbrook (Moorgate to Cannon Street), Effra (Norwood to Vauxhall) and Lower Wandle (Beddington to Wandsworth Town). Three of these were sewerised or canalised while the fourth was neglected (i.e. the Wandle).

7. It is not guaranteed that these pages 'archived' in the Internet Archive Wayback Machine (IAWM) on 14 June 2021 will persist but for now they are available at: https://web.archive.org/web/20210614081955/http://pdms.platformlondon.org/otherprojects.asp#wlf [accessed 12 December 2022].

8. This quotation is from 'Other PLATFORM projects' (no date). An old webpage from Platform's website captured by the IAWM on 14 June 2021 is available at: https://web.archive.org/web/20210614081955/http://pdms.platformlondon.org/otherprojects.asp#wlf [accessed 12 December 2022].

9. Three key projects developed the *Power of the Wandle* sub-project. *The Delta Project* with St. Joseph's RC School was a 1993 project developing the micro-hydro that came out of *Still Waters*. The 1993 *Merton Island Project* on the restoration of the Merton Abbey Mills waterwheel, featured a programme of public events

and engagement on the future of the river and renewables in the area. *Tides and Tributes* was a 1995 residency with four artists in St. Joseph's RC Primary School which was receiving the hydro-electricity from the Wandle. In 1998, Platform was surprised when an 'Effra Liberation Front' surfaced, joining in with a Reclaim the Streets street party.

10. A webpage that escaped the restructuring of the Platform website is Jane Trowell's blog post 'Twenty years ago today: "*Still Waters*", Day 1', posted on 1 May 2012. https://platformlondon. org/2012/05/01/twenty-years-ago-today-still-waters-day-1. Here Trowell states: "Still Waters was given a *Time Out* Award in 1992, and achieved major press coverage in news, environmental and arts media for its innovative approaches. For many years, Platform received a large number of national and international requests across different sectors to run workshops, collaborate, talk, write about the issues and meet with campaigners and engineers who were 'daylighting' buried rivers. We understood that de-sewerising is a whole other infrastructure level to taking the lid off a river that is otherwise flowing normally, and shared the enormity of what had been done to these streams by incorporating them into the sewage system".

11. As of writing, the papers of 'The Museum Of …' temporary museum project are held at the London Metropolitan Archives (LMA). The collection holds material from four of the five 'museums' that together formed *The Museum Of*. These are: *The Museum of Collectors, The Museum of Me, The Museum of Emotions* and *The Museum of the River Thames*. The collection holds no records for *The Museum of the Unknown*. (https://search.lma.gov. uk/scripts/mwimain.dll/144/LMA_OPAC/web_detail?SESSIO NSEARCH&exp=refd%20LMA/4302).

12. See London Metropolitan Archives holding 'THE MUSEUM OF Date of Creation: 1998–2001, Reference Code: LMA/4302' open for public viewing. (https://search.lma.gov.uk/scripts/mwi main.dll/144/LMA_OPAC/web_detail?SESSIONSEARCH& exp=refd%20LMA/4302).

13. See the Internet Archive Wayback Machine screen captures of The Museum Of: https://web.archive.org/web/20010710044652/ http://www.themuseumof.org:80/indexNS.html [accessed 12 December 2022].

14. See UK government webpage 'Thames Water has now accrued £32.4m in fines since 2017 for 11 cases of water pollution' (https://www.gov.uk/government/news/thames-water-fined-4-million-after-30-hour-waterfall-of-sewage-discharge). At the time of writing Thames Water was trending across all UK newspapers

and broadcasters for its level of debt, the departure of its chief executive, regulatory failures and ongoing sewage pollution of rivers (Gill 2023). The biggest investor in Thames Water is the Universities Superannuation Scheme, which has been subject to an ongoing national dispute with the University College Union.

15. https://www.museumoflondon.org.uk/news-room/press-releases/secret-river.

16. *South London Press*, issue 10,039, 12 May 1992. Hard copy photocopy supplied by Jane Trowell, January 2023.

17. https://cargocollective.com/lauraplant/still-water-still.

18. https://www.bishopsgate.org.uk/collections/platform.

19. Museums have storage facilities and basements with sometimes untouched protest memory sources to be reactivated through sustained research and development. For example, Chris Reynolds discovered the only poster of Belfast's 1968 protest, bringing this to the surface and creating new education resources for the GCSE curriculum in Northern Ireland with a 'Voices of "68"' exhibition at Ulster Museum. This is an ongoing project of significant impact in the history curriculum.

20. See Paul Talling's *London's Lost Rivers* book (2011) and website. The Ravensbourne has benefitted from a strategic project (2010–2015) including flood alleviation at Lewisham, citizen science water testing, river clean ups, wade walking, mind mapping and storytelling with London Bubble.

21. See *Heritage From Below* (Robertson 2008, 2012) and Laura Jane Smith's identification of the near-universally accepted Authorised Heritage Discourse (AHD). In stressing the fluidity of both heritage and identity, Smith argues strongly for the understanding of heritage as "something vital and alive … a moment of action" (2006, p. 83). Smith's thesis, therefore, understands heritage as active and processual.

22. For more on river restoration projects, see Smith et al (2014) 'The Changing Nature of River Restoration' and Tricia Cusack (2010) *Riverscapes and National identities*, as well as Schmidt and Mitchell (2013) 'Property and the Right to Water'.

23. During the writing of this chapter numerous news outlets were covering the pollution of English rivers and coasts by private water companies due to their misuse of outdated and inundated Victorian solutions. See Matt Staniek's Windermere Lake Recovery set

up in 2022 as a recent example. In *The Observer* (16 April 2023), the comedian Stewart Lee wrote that "Britain is a dying nation in need of new curators", and the section most reposted on social media concerned rivers: "Every April, I used to go camping on the Wye for the first wild river swim of the year, but this month I have saved money by just shitting and pissing into my own bath and then splashing around in it naked, while wearing a paper mask of the environment secretary, Thérèse Coffey. After I get out, and before towelling down, I issue a misleading statement about how our rivers have never been cleaner to my own bathroom mirror, even though I can still see my own filth tangled in my hair, to the delight of shareholders, and the disappointment of former Undertones singer Feargal Sharkey, unexpectedly emerging from punk cult status as The Most Decent Man In Modern Britain™®. There's no threat of a fine from Brussels any more and Defra is without teeth. Pollute away, polluters!" (Lee 2023).

References

Connerton, P. 2008. Seven Types of Forgetting. *Memory Studies* 1 (1): 59–71.

Cusack, T. 2010. *Riverscapes and National Identities*. Syracuse: Syracuse University Press.

Davies, C. 2021. Network of Green Walks Proposed Along the Routes of London's Forgotten Rivers. *Guardian*, May 4. https://www.theguardian.com/uk-news/2021/may/04/network-of-green-walks-proposed-along-routes-of-londons-forgotten-rivers. Accessed 20 Apr 2023.

De Sousa Santos, B. 2014. *Epistemologies of the South: Justice against Epistemicide*. London: Routledge.

Garde-Hansen, J. 2021. *Media and Water Communication, Culture and Perception*. London: I.B. Tauris.

Garde-Hansen, J., L. McEwen, A. Holmes, and O. Jones. 2016. Sustainable Flood Memory: Remembering as Resilience. *Memory Studies* 10 (4): 384–405.

Ghosh, A. 2016. *The Great Derangement Climate Change and the Unthinkable*. Chicago: Chicago University Press.

Gill, O. 2023. University Pension Scheme Braced for Wipeout of Biggest Investment if Thames Water Collapses. *The Telegraph*, June 29. https://www.telegraph.co.uk/business/2023/06/29/university-pension-scheme-braced-for-wipeout-thames-water. Accessed 1 Jul 2023.

ICOM. 2022. Statement: Museums and Climate Activism. https://icom.mus eum/en/news/icom-statement-climate-activism. Accessed 1 Dec 2022.

Illich, I. 1985. *H₂O and the Waters of Forgetfulness*. Dallas: Dallas Institute of Humanities and Culture.

Lee, S. 2023. Britain is a Dying Nation in Need for New Curators. *The Observer*, April 16. https://www.theguardian.com/commentisfree/2023/apr/16/bri tain-is-a-dying-nation-in-need-of-new-curators. Accessed 20 Apr 2023.

Lejano, R., J. Tavares-Reager, and F. Berkes. 2013. Climate and Narrative: Environmental Knowledge in Everyday Life. *Environmental Science and Policy* 31: 61–70.

Nixon, R. 2011. *Slow Violence and the Environmentalism of the Poor*. Cambridge: Harvard University Press.

Robertson, I. 2008. Heritage from Below: Class, Social Protest and Resistance. In *The Ashgate Research Companion to Heritage and Identity*, ed. B. Graham and P. Howard, 143–158. Farnham: Ashgate.

Robertson, I., ed. 2012. *Heritage from Below*. Farnham: Ashgate.

Schmidt, J., and K. Mitchell. 2013. Property and the Right to Water. *Review of Radical Political Economics* 46 (1): 54–69.

Serafini, P. 2022. *Creating Worlds Otherwise: Art, Collective Action, and (Post) Extractivism*. Nashville: Vanderbilt University Press.

Smith, B, N. Clifford, and J. Mant. 2014. The Changing Nature of River Restoration. *WIREs Water* 1 (3): 249–261.

Smith, L.J. 2006. *Uses of Heritage*. London: Routledge.

Talling, P. 2011. *London's Lost Rivers*. London: Penguin.

Tavory, I., and R. Wagner-Pacifici. 2022. Climate Change as an Event. *Poetics* 93: 101600. https://doi.org/10.1016/j.poetic.2021.101600.

Wild, T.C., J.F. Bernet, E.L. Westling, and D.N. Lerner. 2011. Deculverting: Reviewing the Evidence on the 'Daylighting' and Restoration of Culverted Rivers. *Water and Environment Journal* 25 (3): 412–421.

CHAPTER 6

Reflections on Precarity and Risk

Abstract In this chapter we summarise key insights from our study and introduce important reflections from the *Afterlives of Protest Research Network* to further the work of academics and practitioners in the field. We discuss the significant role of holistic accountability within the cultural sector and the emergent role of digital technologies in expanding public understandings of protest memory beyond the purely aesthetic. We situate the ethical challenges that sit behind the imperative to tell 'both sides of the story' of protest histories and demonstrate how institutional power can problematically be reinscribed through uncompensated activist labour. Encompassing these concerns is an attention to issues of precarity and risk with the cultural, arts and heritage sector.

Keywords Protest memory · Accountability · Hate studies · Cultural labour · Digital technologies

Moving beyond established understandings of 'protest memory' as social movements that are socially and culturally remembered in society through acts of representation and commemoration, this book has set forward a new analytical framework. We have explored how protest memory operates as a theme, method and active ethos within the cultural, arts and heritage sector. As one of the first academic works to take a sustained look at the activist politics of museums and archives through a memory lens, we have examined:

- How museums and archives collect, display and interpret protest cultures, both historic and of the present, with increasing social justice intent;
- How connections can be made between social movements, and across eras and geographies through cultural memory practices;
- How the media-memory-activism nexus underpins the collection, curation and contestation of protest memories in the public sphere;
- How public museums and archives enact protest from within and outside their walls—not only through collecting and curating protest materials, but by bringing protest techniques, knowledge and orientations into their mission statements and operating values;
- How cultural institutions engage in acts of museum, archival and memory activism, including through collaborating, supporting and providing resources and space for local community and activist groups;
- How protest memory draws on a variety of mnemonic rhythms, from rapid response and anticipatory memorialisation to the sustained mnemonic attention required to protect and care for protest memory over the long term.

Our evocation of 'protest memory' in this book has served to investigate four main analytical terrains. First, to understand how social movements, activist cultures and mass eruptions of protest in the public sphere are being approached by mainstream, institutional museums and archives in this current conjuncture. We sought to establish what is being collected and curated, how and with what claims to cultural value and significance. Second, to understand the wider processes of decision-making that museum, archive and activist-practitioners undertake in practice, including their creative, technological and innovative strategies in engaging with the actors, materials and mnemonic traces of protest. Within this terrain, we have examined how 'power-sharing' happens within the cultural sector on the topic of protest (such as strategies of co-creation and co-production) and how wider audiences and publics are being involved. Third, we called into question how this memory work is considered as 'activist', or not, by its institutional actors, placing our empirical case studies into conversation with the emerging and established concepts of 'museum activism' (Janes and Sandell 2019), 'archival activism' (Flinn 2011) and 'memory activism' (Gutman and Wüstenberg 2023). Finally, we drew these concerns together to consider how museum and archive engagements with contemporary protesters, social movements and civic actors—and the causes they mobilise and advocate for—shines a necessary spotlight on the institutional frameworks and practices of cultural institutions themselves.

This study was supported by the activities of the *Afterlives of Protest Research Network,* funded by the Arts and Humanities Research Council (2018–2019). During this series of expert workshops, keynotes, conference presentations and networking opportunities between academics, cultural and heritage workers, activists and artists, it became clear that there was an appetite for engaging in social justice and social change work. This desire spoke to a wish to bridge traditional divides between formal and informal knowledge, but with the need for more guidance to steer the collaborations, policies and methods that such relationships would require. Since the launch of our network, we are pleased to have witnessed a surge in toolkits providing sector guidance on contemporary and rapid response collecting (Fredheim et al. 2018; Kavanagh 2019; Miles et al. 2020), the curation of social justice exhibitions (Gonzales 2020) and archiving social media and born digital records (Jules et al. 2018; University of Virginia Library 2019).

Engaging with protest memory by necessity shines a light on the wider work that the collecting-archiving-curatorial institution is doing to uphold social justice values and to make their institutions truly accessible and accountable to diverse publics and communities of interest. This is difficult work in the context of funding challenges, reputational risk (Cameron and Kelly 2010) and ongoing culture wars, where sites of history-making and memory are weaponised by dominant power structures (Dubin 2011; MacDonald 1998). To engage with a protest memory ethos and orientation takes courage and dedication. This leads us to consider issues of precarity when it comes to protest memory and the agency of cultural institutions. As Nicholas Ridout and Rebecca Schneider determine (2012, p. 5), precarity:

is life lived in relation to a future that cannot be propped securely upon the past. Precarity undoes a linear streamline of temporary progression and challenges 'progress' and 'development' narratives on all levels.

We see precarity operating on several scales in the realm of protest memory. Protest cultures and protest gains are precarious and can be subjected to legislative roll backs[1]; protest memories are precarious and easily forgotten or erased unless carefully tended to; the funding streams of museums and archives are precarious and can put institutions in jepodary[2]; and precarity is a by-word for many (cultural) workers' conditions and contracts under neoliberal late capitalism, where livelihoods are made vulnerable due to project-based and freelance work.

During our work in the *Afterlives of Protest Research Network* and in writing this book, we have witnessed multiple precarities in terms of protest, memory and the livelihood of the cultural sector, where the impact of the Covid-19 pandemic and the current cost-of-living crisis has served to exacerbate existing inequalities. While we have witnessed a veritable 'memory boom' in institutional projects around protest, memory, activism and advocacy over the past decade, we have also observed worrying threats to human rights, dignity and democratic rights to protest. There is no overarching, linear narrative of social change. Struggles long fought for and won can be eroded and pushed back; new gains in cultural visibility for historically marginalised groups are met with increased hate crimes and violence on the ground. As we worked on this book, the UK government pushed through new legislation to curtail the right to protest. This adds the UK to an increasing number of state authorities expanding measures to suppress organised dissent—including Russia, Sri Lanka, France, Senegal, Iran and Nicaragua.[3]

The UK's new Public Order Bill, ratified in 2023, grants police enforcement agencies expanded powers to stop and search protesters with no grounds of suspicion required; to dismantle protests for being 'too noisy' and to pre-emptively dismantle protests in case they became disruptive; to ban slow walking as a method of disruption; and to issue individuals with a protest ban. Further restrictions include criminalising peaceful protest tactics such as 'locking on' to equipment and infrastructures and blocking roads and traffic. By rationale, the UK government offers a discursive appeal to the act of balancing the right to protest with the right of the public to go about their business.[4] On closer inspection, this translates to the right for *business as usual* without the 'disruptive costs' of protest—especially when climate emergency protesters target infrastructure and corporations, including airports, to protest business as usual thinking.

Our book has centred the argument that protest memory is connective: it connects social justice movements, citizens, policymakers, cultural and heritage workers, academics, artists and communities (we intentionally omit the word stakeholders because of its colonial roots).[5] Of course, protest memories are contentious and divisive. How to hold space for multiple, conflicting views and experiences is a skill set necessary for today's professional cultural, heritage and memory workers. This has been approached productively by our network participants through the idea of creating 'brave spaces' rather than 'safe spaces'.[6] A protest memory ethos and orientation, as we have proposed in this book and explored through our case studies, challenges and innovates the operational work of museums and archives on the ground. To conclude, we would like to share four final reflections that emerged from our research network that we hope can be useful for academics and practitioners alike.

The first is the notion of *holistic accountability* on the side of the cultural institution, and the difficulties of achieving this. From an activist perspective, it is not enough to hold temporary exhibitions on protest while simultaneously benefitting from systems of power and capital which activists fight against (for example, cultural sector struggles for fair pay and secure contracts, to eradicate institutional racism and colonial knowledge systems, and to think through the amplification and representation of underserved communities, including working-class professionals and audiences). The issue of holistic accountability was clearly demonstrated through the case of the Design Museum, London in 2018, in relation to their exhibition *Hope to Nope: Graphics and Politics 2008–2018*. This exhibition showcased political art from the past decade. In July 2018, over 30 artists—a third of those represented in the exhibition—demanded that the museum remove their work following the Design Museum hosting a trade event from one of the world's largest defence companies, Leonardo.[7] An open letter posted on the *Campaign Against Arms Trade* website and signed by participating artists stated in no uncertain terms:

> It is deeply hypocritical for the museum to display and celebrate the work of radical anti-corporate artists and activists, while quietly supporting and profiting from one of the most destructive and deadly industries in the world.

> *Hope to Nope* is making the museum appear progressive and cutting-edge, while its management and trustees are happy to take blood money from arms dealers.

> We refuse to allow our art to be used in this way.

> (Frearson 2018)

These statements demonstrate that such hypocrisy is untenable from an activist point of view, underscored by the perspective that museums draw cultural prestige from engaging in activism-washing. From their side, the directors of the Design Museum posted a letter on the museum's website in response (Sudjic and Black 2018). The tenor of this statement is to emphasise the popularity of the exhibition (30,000 visitors at the time of the statement), and to issue a claim for political neutrality: "[The exhibition] presents a range of views, from across the political spectrum. Our objective was never to side with any party or world view, but to show how different sides have expressed their beliefs, through design". The statement continues: "As an educational charity, we cannot take an overt political stance as some activists would like us to do. Recent events have shown us that breaching the laws that regulate charities could put us at risk of having our charitable status removed [...] There are clear rules for charities regarding political activity that form a key part of both charity law and public expectations".

In a somewhat unfortunate response to the boycott, the museum directors went on to disparage "Professional activists whose work didn't feature in the exhibition [who] took the view that the museum had acted wrongfully and were quick to exploit the situation". While conceding that the Design Museum will review event hire policies, the overarching tone is one of institutional victimisation and defiance: "We are a charity which receives barely 2% of its funding from the public purse [...] The long term impact of these protests will be to reduce the work that we do which is designed to benefit the sector and the wider public". This is coupled with the rigid stance: "The outcome of these protests will be to censor the exhibition, curtail free speech and prevent the museum from showcasing a plurality of views". While not diminishing the very real restrictions placed on cultural institutions as charities and organisations facing significant funding pressures, there appears a missed opportunity here and a discursive sleight of hand. A more productive response, perhaps, could be to acknowledge the real tensions and conflicts at work, but to demonstrate a commitment to institutional reflexivity and change.

The second take away point from the network was a concern with *how protest could be reduced to aesthetics*—or pure visual culture—within the GLAM and heritage sectors. Design clearly has an important role in activism as a way of conveying messages, capturing public attention and creating collective imaginaries. The creative and cultural work within social movements and activist cultures are notable parts of their function and impact.[8] However, network participants expressed a concern that much can be lost when only aesthetics and material cultures are attended to, including the potential loss of wider social lives of protest, or what Harvie and Milburn (2006) refer to as "moments of excess". Such moments speak to the visceral, bodily experiences, whether banal or spectacular, in micro or macro events, that involve intense or small forms of creativity and cooperation with others, and through which other worlds seem possible. This speaks to the networks, relationships, emotions, trajectories and subjectivities that make protest possible; this concern is very much about how to bring 'people' into protest display and how to incubate 'political feelings', 'creative citizens' and 'disobedient institutions'.

In previous chapters we examined alternative forms of curation (Chapter 3), including crowd-sourced collections and rapid response collecting and curation (Chapter 4). We considered techniques of re-exhibition (Chapter 5), innovations in display and labels (Chapter 3), and putting artefacts, causes and civic actors in dialogue with each other across movements, geographies and time in an assemblage approach (Chapter 4). What remains is how to achieve even more layers and nuances of conflict and contestation, without resulting in information overload for the visitor, and potentially in ways in which visitors themselves become active agents within the remembering of protest cultures. We recommend considering how digital technologies can enable more mobile and motile protest memories, such as the use of QR codes within labels and displays to take the visitor to another website with further information (especially presenting background information, or the stories of contention behind any particular artefact, technique or event).[9] QR codes could be used to unlock protest playlists to accompany exhibitions, or YouTube playlists, or an exhibition blog or institutional social media account that further highlights audio-visual content.

Over the years we have noticed that museums and galleries often follow the temptation to present information on activism through a mimicking of protest placards (we have done this ourselves, with our protest network logo and book front cover). It is a seductive route, to echo the protest aesthetics it draws from, but one that can be of limited success. While useful as a low-budget solution, we encourage museums to think in more generative and infrastructural ways in how high-spec and interactive technologies could be used to present protest histories innovatively: from augmented reality, virtual reality and emerging web 3.0 technologies to interactive displays to open new forms of engagement with the details and specifics of individual protesters, groups and acts. Afterall, within the scope of protest memory we can also include the memorability generated in the visitor, which they will carry away with them. Embodied protest memories, facilitated through display, immersion, pedagogical activities, curated storytelling, acts of movement and engagement, haptic encounters, spaces for rest and joy, moments of reflection, 'sightlines' and 'soundlines' to resistance following the presentation of violence and trauma, are important elements. As Gonzales (2020, p. 59) notes, exhibitions "for social justice are more effective when they combine resonance and emotion". Laughter and playfulness in particular help to create the conditions for memorability in individuals; these are techniques ripe to be explored further in protest memory curation and re-activation. As Gonzales (2020, p. 82) instructs, potential curators should ask: what do you want your audiences to know, to feel and to do?

A third reflection emerging from the research network was the *difficulties surrounding collecting and representing histories 'from both sides' of a struggle.* At times these sides appear clear-cut, such as the Repeal the 8th campaign in Ireland in 2018. This campaign returned an overwhelming 'yes vote' in the referendum to overturn the 8th amendment of the Irish constitution, which, since 1983, instituted the "right to life of the unborn" and an abortion ban. During an expert workshop on curating protest memories for our network, Kate Antosik-Parsons, an academic and steering committee member of the Archiving the 8th initiative, discussed the archiving difficulties of quickly responding to the referendum, seeking to collect not only from the manifestly 'yes' and 'no' campaigns (including artworks, publications, activist strategies, social media conversations and mainstream media responses), but also from the 'reluctant yes', 'the silent yes' and undecided voters (Antosik-Parsons 2019). Discussing the challenges of volunteer-led rapid response collecting, Antosik-Parsons detailed

how "many of the campaign groups have disappeared. It's also difficult to source participation from the no campaign, even though their
perspectives and materials are vital for collection purposes". Sometimes
unconventional methods are called for, such as the curator of the National
Museum of Ireland, Brenda Malone, who took to the streets following the
referendum to cut placards from lampposts for the museum's archive—
including a banner depicting a foetus with the slogan: Don't repeal me
(Marshall 2018).

How to collect, display and interpret such contentious materials is
an ongoing challenge for archivists, curators, and heritage workers. This
is a fraught ethical terrain that is still being discussed. Several practitioners within our network stated that they wouldn't create exhibitions
from heated national referendums (such as Brexit and Repeal the 8th),
until more time had passed, until they had gained sufficient material
to represent a breadth of perspectives, and until they were clearer on
how to approach interpretation. Taking this perspective further leads us
to consider whether, and if so, how, museums and memory institutions
should engage with what Kylie Message (2022) aptly calls the "citizenship
of hate". Recognising that the recent activist turn in the GLAM sector
prioritises activism from a social justice and left perspective, Message
queries in what ways national museums "have an obligation to engage
with a broad spectrum of political participation and expression, including
contemporary forms of far-right extremism and white grievance politics"
(2022, p. 2).

Noting that the goal for such work would be to equip institutions and
publics with knowledge to better understand the impact of hate crimes
and to take a stand against the culture of fear it generates, Message grap-
ples with how to do so without providing a platform for such ideas and
actors. Seeking to raise questions rather than to provide answers, Message
points to how museums are themselves targets of hate speech acts—
including a noose (a symbol of white racial terror) left at the National
Museum of African American History and Culture (Boissoneault 2017).
These too, she contends, are forms of citizen activism, even if they represent the most unpalatable, despicable and antisocial ones. Message points
to the growth of a new academic field in 'hate studies' to further direct
such museological concerns. She also clarifies that the aim of such curatorial activism would be to rehumanise victims of hate speech, to underscore
the intersections of hate in relation to power, social status, race, gender
and so forth, and to spotlight what specific social structures and forms of

media, communication and representation allow hate speech to become ubiquitous and normalised.

This brings us to the final reflection that emerged from the *Afterlives of Protest Research Network*, summed up by the phrase from an activist participant: *follow the money to understand power*. Much co-creation work in museums is predicated on volunteer labour from community members. However, activists are increasingly demanding to be seen as cultural workers who deserve financial compensation for their time and expertise. During our network project, we had not originally included participation fees for activists in our budget (and note that these costs may not have been permitted by the funder), only travel and hospitality costs. This excluded some from participating. For others, we managed to secure additional university funding to pay small honorariums for their participation and for contributions to this book, which was done in an unsatisfactory ad hoc fashion because it was not budgeted from the beginning. These fees were either donated back to the organisations the activists were part of or were used by activists who are freelancers and/or who appreciated the compensation in terms of their labour insecurity. Compensation can also be extended to cultural workers within the GLAM sector. Here we take inspiration from Robenalt, Farrell-Banks and Markham, editors of the *Journal of Museum Education* special issue on activist pedagogies (2022). They recognise that structural inequalities frame museal and educational institutions, which impact who gets to speak and who is compensated. Finding no readily available guidelines on how much to pay non-academics for their contributions to the academic community, these scholars used the National Union of Journalists Freelance Fees Guide to calculate how much to pay practitioners for their contributions to the journal.[10] As they argue, all too often "those working hard to identify and amend the inequalities we see are asked to labor for the benefit of others without acknowledging the difficulties and time involved" (Robenalt et al. 2022, p. 405).[11]

In this vein, we view the memory work involved in identifying, collecting, preserving, making accessible and interpreting protest material culture and networks as being difficult, but crucial, forms of cultural labour in which practitioners—often without institutional guidelines and policies—innovate as they go. We hope a key contribution of this book is to better understand and celebrate how mainstream and establishment museums and archives—as memory institutions, not just as cultural institutions—act as powerful sites, sources, agents, caretakers and innovators of social movement knowledge and legacies. This is alongside their role as institutions reckoning with historic, ongoing and systemic inequities. We note that not all institutional responses to social movements are equal, and not all have been convincing: the accountability audit by activists and cultural practitioners pertaining to Black Lives Matter pledges by art institutions following the George Floyd protests is a case in point (Dafoe and Goldstein 2020).

We conclude with a powerful recognition of the physical, emotional, time-rich and fiscal costs that activists and activist-practitioners endure as individuals and collectives, as the frontline and shock absorbers of social justice agitation. Activists and disruptors labour to make new worlds liveable (not only visitable). They stand within a shifting horizon of past-present-future memory actions and issue potent reminders of the unfinished business of social justice projects today. To talk of history in institutional contexts can often suggest an event or struggle is relegated to the past, that it is over and done with. To evoke memory alongside history is to keep these struggles open, alive and subject to intervention. The concept of *protest memory* introduced in this book has been issued with such an intention. We envision that academics and practitioners will continue this difficult yet vital, ongoing work, informed by the knowledge practices, artful care, joy, innovations and demands for ethical living drawn from disobedient protest cultures. There is much still to explore in how museums and archives can further social justice futurity, and the creative ways in which mediated, digital and embodied protest memories can guide this work.

NOTES

1. In June 2022, the US Supreme Court voted to end fifty years of reproductive rights protection when they struck down Roe v. Wade; ruling that women no longer had a constitutional right to abortion. In the US, queer communities have been placed under new attack, with 15 conservative states introducing laws in 2023 which prohibit or restrict drag shows and target trans* communities.
2. One of the book's central case studies, the People's History Museum (PHM), was cited in a debate in the House of Lords on the issue of precarious museum funding; the PHM was the only national museum without secure future income

streams (https://hansard.parliament.uk/lords/2015-01-26/26/ debates/15012629000134/Museums Funding). The loss of income during the Covid-19 pandemic provided further precarity for the PHM, who, in turn, created a successful public crowd-funding campaign to help secure their future (www.crowdfunder. co.uk/p/futurephm).

3. In July 2022, Amnesty International launched a global campaign to confront the unprecedented worldwide threat to the right to protest (https://www.amnesty.org/en/latest/news/2022/07/ protect-the-protest).

4. https://www.gov.uk/government/publications/public-order-bill-overarching-documents/public-order-bill-factsheet.

5. There have been debates within the US, Canada and Australia over the offensiveness of the term 'stakeholder' in relation to First Nations and indigenous peoples. During the colonial process, 'stakeholders' referred to settlers who used wooden stakes to claim land prior to any treaty or land negotiations, resulting in land theft and dispossession (https://www2.gov.bc.ca/gov/content/ governments/services-for-government/service-experience-digital-delivery/web-content-development-guides/web-style-guide/wri ting-guide-for-indigenous-content/terminology#outdated-terms).

6. Arao and Clemens define brave spaces as those that "emphasize the need for courage rather than the illusion of safety" (2013, p. 141). Tate Exchange (2016–2021), a five-year programme at Tate Modern, London, positioned itself as a "brave, risk-taking" space aimed at fostering "new thinking on the museum". Tate Exchange explored annual themes (exchange, production, move-ment, power, love) in experimental ways with Tate colleagues, community associate organisations, artists and visitors. It had a dedicated floor at Tate Modern and enacted a unique platform that combined curation, education and social participation (https:// www.tate.org.uk/tate-exchange).

7. The artists who withdrew their work from *Hope to Nope*, mounted a free exhibition *From Hope to Nope: Art vs Arms, Oil and Injustice* (2018) at Brixton Recreation Centre. Charlie Waterhouse, one of the exhibition organisers and exhibiting artists spoke to the alter-native magazine *Good Trouble* of the constraints of exhibiting in mainstream museum spaces, echoing perspectives from museum staff explored in Chapter 4: "a lot of the artists had difficulty seeing

their work in that kind of rarified atmosphere. The white walls, entrance fee and Kensington location are all a bit of an anathema. The setting immediately separated the work from the reality of the activism" (Waterhouse 2018). On the anniversary of the *Hope to Nope* boycott, the Nope to Arms Collective published a statement outlining corporate conflicts of interests with the Design Museum's chair of trustees, who had business interests in a Russian defence firm and BP as a consultancy client. The collective also drew attention to the lack of follow-up action of the Design Museum reviewing its private hire policies. The statement proceeds to outline several high-profile examples from the cultural sector where ethical sponsorship policies have been adhered to. The very act of holding cultural institutions to account for pledges made can be viewed as another form of *protest memory* within the cultural sector (https://cultureunstained.org/a-statement-from-nope-to-arms).

8. While activist art and aesthetics form a key part of protest memory, movements can also become constrained in producing such outputs. For a discussion of the use of A4 blank pieces of paper as protest signs in geopolitical contexts in which protest is highly surveilled and censored, such as China and Russia, see Perrigo (2022). For a survey of the aesthetics of global protest see Aidan et al. (2019). For a critical take on the aestheticisation of politics, in relation to fascism, capitalism, spectacle and the 'distribution of the sensible', alongside aesthetics' political potential and its ability to re-envision the space–time sensibilities of the (postcolonial) museum, see Ferris (2009) and Tolia-Kelly (2019).

9. We recognise that digital and connective technologies come with their own accessibility challenges in museum spaces. Researchers have attended to the possibilities and challenges of QR code use in museums since their inception in the early 2000s (Schultz 2013). Technology is evolving and some of the constraints of QR use are being displaced with the integration of QR readers within smartphones, plus the significant use of QR codes during the Covid-19 pandemic has strengthened user familiarity. Two-way QR codes have also been developed which enable users to leave comments and interact with linked content, thus encompassing a social aspect rather than one-way information transfer. For a summary of how QR codes can be successfully integrated into exhibitions and displays, see Coulson (2022).

10. https://www.nuj.org.uk/advice/freelance-resources.html.
11. While a benefit of rapid response and contemporary collecting is that artefacts of the present can be acquired at a cost-effective price or for free by archives and museums, this creates ethical challenges in the context of activist-made art. For example, the Whitney Museum of American Art in New York purchased several artworks by Black creatives at a highly discounted price via a charity fundraiser in 2020. The Whitney had aimed to exhibit these works at a planned exhibition of activist art in response to the pandemic and Black Lives Matter protests, yet without the artists' consent or compensation. Following backlash for unethical and exploitative practices, the museum cancelled the show (Rea 2020).

REFERENCES

Aidan, M., I. Erhart, H. Eslen-Ziya, O. Jenzen, and U. Korkut (eds.). 2019. *The Aesthetics of Global Protest*. Amsterdam: Amsterdam University Press. https://library.oapen.org/handle/20.500.12657/23606. Accessed 20 Apr 2023.

Antosik-Parsons, K. 2019. Archiving the 8th. Panel—Protest Objects and Rapid Response Collecting. *Curating Protest Memory Expert Workshop,* March 28. King's College London.

Arao, B., and K. Clemens. 2013. From Safe Spaces to Brave Spaces: A New Way to Frame Dialogue Around Diversity and Social Justice. In *The Art of Effective Facilitation: Reflections from Social Justice Educators,* ed. L.M. Landreman, 135–150. Sterling: Stylus.

Boissoneault, L. 2017. Noose Found in National Museum of African American History and Culture. *Smithsonian Magazine,* May 31. https://www.smithsonianmag.com/smithsonian-institution/noose-found-national-museum-african-american-history-and-culture-180963519. Accessed 20 Apr 2023.

Cameron, F., and L. Kelly (eds.). 2010. *Hot Topics, Public Culture, Museums.* Newcastle upon Tyne: Cambridge Scholars.

Coulson, A. 2022. QR Codes in Museums—Worth the Effort? *National Museums Scotland,* July 19. https://blog.nms.ac.uk/2022/07/19/qr-codes-in-museums-worth-the-effort. Accessed 20 Apr 2023.

Dafoe, T., and C. Goldstein. 2020. The George Floyd Protests Spurred Museums to Promise Change. Here's What They've Actually Done So Far. *Artnet,* August 14. https://news.artnet.com/art-world/museums-diversity-equity-commitments-1901564. Accessed 20 Apr 2023.

Dubin, S. 2011. Incivilities in Civil(-ized) Places: 'Culture Wars' in Comparative Perspectives. In *A Companion to Museum Studies*, ed. S. Macdonald, 477–493. Chichester: Wiley-Blackwell.

Ferris, D. 2009. Politics after Aesthetics: Disagreeing with Rancière. *Parallax* 15 (3): 37–49.

Flinn, A. 2011. Archival Activism: Independent and Community-Led Archives, Radical Public History and the Heritage Professions. *InterActions: UCLA Journal of Education and Information Studies* 7 (2). https://doi.org/10.5070/D472000699. Accessed 9 Oct 2022.

Frearson, A. 2018. Designers Demand Design Museum Remove Works in Outrage Over Arms Industry Event. *Dezeen,* July 30. www.dezeen.com/2018/07/30/design-museum-hope-to-nope-arms-event-outrage. Accessed 20 Apr 2023.

Fredheim, H., S. Macdonald, and J. Morgan. 2018. *Profusion in Museums. A Report on Contemporary Collecting and Disposal.* https://heritage-futures.org/profusion-in-museums-report. Accessed 20 Apr 2023.

Gonzales, E. 2020. *Exhibitions for Social Justice.* New York: Routledge.

Gutman, Y., and J. Wüstenberg (eds.). 2023. *The Routledge Companion of Memory Activism.* New York: Routledge.

Harvie, D., and K. Milburn. 2006. *Moments of Excess.* University of Leicester. https://hdl.handle.net/2381/2679. Accessed 20 Apr 2023.

Janes, R.R., and R. Sandell (eds.). 2019. *Museum Activism.* London: Routledge.

Jules, B., E. Summers., and V. Mitchell. 2018. *Documenting the Now White Paper. Ethical Considerations for Archiving Social Media Content Generated by Contemporary Social Movements.* https://www.docnow.io/docs/docnow-whitepaper-2018.pdf. Accessed 20 Apr 2023.

Kavanagh, J. 2019. *Contemporary Collecting Toolkit.* https://museumdevelopmentnorthwest.files.wordpress.com/2019/07/mdnw_contemporarycollectingtoolkit_july2019.pdf. Accessed 20 Apr 2023.

Macdonald, S. (ed.). 1998. *The Politics of Display: Museums, Science, Culture.* London: Routledge.

Marshall, A. 2018. Posters, Banners, Boarding Passes: Museums Try to Get a Head Start on History. *The New York Times,* June 18. https://www.nytimes.com/2018/06/18/arts/design/rapid-response-collecting-ireland-berlin.html. Accessed 20 Apr 2023.

Message, K. 2022. Museums and the Citizenship of Hate. *Museum Worlds* 10 (1): 1–13.

Miles, E., S. Cordner, and J. Kavanagh (eds.). 2020. Contemporary Collecting. An Ethical Toolkit for Museum Practitioners. https://collectionstrust.org.uk/resource/contemporary-collecting-toolkit-2. Accessed 20 Apr 2023.

Perrigo, B. 2022. Why a Blank Sheet of Paper Became a Protest Symbol in China. *Time*, December 1. https://time.com/6238050/china-protests-censorship-urumqi-a4. Accessed 20 Apr 2023.

Rea, N. 2020. Following Heated Online Protests, the Whitney has Cancelled a Planned Exhibition Featuring Lockdown-Era Works It Bought at Charity Auctions. *Artnet*, August 26. https://news.artnet.com/art-world/whitney-museum-collective-actions-1904266. Accessed 20 Apr 2023.

Robenalt, E., D. Farrell-Banks, and K. Markham. 2022. Activist Pedagogies in Museum Studies and Practice: A Critical Reflection. *Journal of Museum Education* 47 (4): 401–413.

Ridout, N., and R. Schneider. 2012. Precarity and Performance: An Introduction. *The Drama Review* 56 (4): 5–9.

Schultz, M.K. 2013. A Case Study on the Appropriateness of Using Quick Response (QR) Codes in Libraries and Museums. *Library and Information Science Research* 35 (3): 207–215.

Sudjic, D., and A. Black. 2018. A Letter about Hope to Nope: Graphics and Politics 2008–2018. https://designmuseum.org/press-office/a-letter-about-hope-to-nope-graphics-and-politics-2008-18. Accessed 20 Apr 2023.

Tolia-Kelly, D. 2019. Rancière and the Re-distribution of the Sensible: The Artist Rosanna Raymond, Dissensus and Postcolonial Sensibilities Within the Spaces of the Museum. *Progress in Human Geography* 43 (1): 123–140.

University of Virginia Library. 2019. *Digital Collecting Toolkit*. http://digitalcollecting.lib.virginia.edu/toolkit/toolkit_7_29_19.pdf. Accessed 20 Apr 2023.

Waterhouse, C. 2018. From Nope to Hope. *Good Trouble*, October 4. www.goodtroublemag.com/home/nope-to-hope-art-against-arms. Accessed 20 Apr 2023.

INDEX

GPSR Compliance

The European Union's (EU) General Product Safety Regulation (GPSR) is a set of rules that requires consumer products to be safe and our obligations to ensure this.

If you have any concerns about our products, you can contact us on ProductSafety@springernature.com

In case Publisher is established outside the EU, the EU authorized representative is:

Springer Nature Customer Service Center GmbH
Europaplatz 3
69115 Heidelberg, Germany

The manufacturer's authorised representative in the EU is Springer
Nature Customer Service Centre GmbH, Europaplatz 3, 69115 Heidelberg,
Germany. If you have any concerns regarding our products, please
contact ProductSafety@springernature.com

Printed and bound by CPI Group (UK) Ltd, Croydon, CR0 4YY
24/04/2026
02096362-0003